*From*

A L M O S T

*to*

ALTOGETHER

*From*

| A | L | M | O | S | T |
|---|---|---|---|---|---|

*to*

ALTOGETHER

*Sermons on Christian Discipleship*

JOHN WESLEY

The John Wesley Collection
Andrew C. Thompson
Executive Editor

# CONTENTS

*Publisher's Foreword* vii

*Acknowledgments* ix

*Introduction* xi

1. The Circumcision of the Heart 3

2. The Almost Christian 19

3. The First-Fruits of the Spirit 31

4. The Way to the Kingdom 47

5. Marks of the New Birth 61

6. On Sin in Believers 77

7. The Repentance of Believers 95

8. The Good Steward 117

9. The More Excellent Way 137

# PUBLISHER'S FOREWORD

John Wesley's profound legacy and impact on world Christianity in his lifetime and since can be viewed through several lenses. The revival that arose under his leadership changed the social and political structure of eighteenth-century England as the poor and lost found hope in the gospel of Jesus Christ rather than in revolution against the crown. The influence of Wesley's Spirit-inspired teaching continued unabated as the Methodist movement spread scriptural holiness across the American continent and lands far beyond.

Wesley's influence as a publisher represents an astonishing record in its own right. Wesley lived in a time when Gutenberg's invention of movable type, which had immediately preceded Luther's reformation, had coalesced into specialized printing trades in London. Typefounders and printeries offered exciting new pathways for the spread of the gospel through inexpensive printed text.

Perhaps more than any other figure of his day, Wesley embraced this new technology and issued sermons, tracts, commentaries, abridgments, biographies, and a host of other items that he considered relevant to the spiritual growth of maturing Christians.

Wesley was vitally driven by the reality of the inner witness of the Holy Spirit. His teaching on entire sanctification, or Christian perfection, is the capstone of his legacy. He worked tirelessly to abridge and republish seminal works by historical figures of previous generations, reaching as far back as the apostolic fathers of the first-century church. He constantly curated voices that communicated the work of the Holy Spirit in bringing believers into the fullness of salvation and lives of holy love.

These writings resourced the early Methodists in their quest to spread the gospel by providing the intellectual and spiritual moorings for the messengers of the movement. Seedbed believes these writings are as relevant today as they were in the eighteenth and nineteenth centuries.

With great joy we present The John Wesley Collection. In the years ahead, Seedbed will reissue selections from this vast collection, which includes his fifty-volume Christian Library, some 150 sermons, countless items from his journals and letters, as well as innumerable tracts, hymns, poems, and other publications, most of which have been out of circulation for decades, if not centuries. We encourage you to enter these texts with determination. Readers who persevere will soon find themselves accustomed to the winsome tenor and tempo of Wesley's voice and vernacular.

Seedbed's editors are constantly examining the more than 250 years of vital spiritual writing by Wesley and successive generations to find the most relevant and helpful messages that will speak to today's body of believers. We commend this old-new publishing work to you as one ready to be transformed by the latent power of these ancient truths. It is our prayer that these timeless words will add fuel to the fire of an awakening ready to ignite once again across the world.

*Sola sancta caritas!* Amen.

Andrew Miller
Seedbed Publishing

# ACKNOWLEDGMENTS

The text for each of John Wesley's sermons included in this compilation originally came from the online Christian Classics Ethereal Library.

The sermons in Chapters 2–4 were edited anonymously at the Memorial University of Newfoundland. The sermons in Chapters 1 and 5–7 were initially edited by students at Northwest Nazarene College: Dave Giles, Jennifer Vail, Angel Miller, Anita Maendl. The sermon in Chapter 8 came from umcmission.org. The sermon in Chapter 9 was initially edited by Pastor Edward Purkey.

George Lyons of Northwest Nazarene College (Nampa, Idaho) made additional corrections to the sermons in Chapters 1–7 and 9 for the Wesley Center for Applied Theology.

# INTRODUCTION

John Wesley wanted more than anything that those under his care would experience the joy of true holiness. He believed that present salvation is a gift God offers to all people, and he referred to this gift as *holiness of heart and life*. He even believed that holiness was the reason God called his brother Charles and him into the leadership of a movement for which, in many ways, they were ill suited. Looking back on the beginning of the Methodist revival in the late 1730s, Wesley once sketched an image of two young men who were more interested in academic pursuits and the salvation of their own souls than anything else. To their surprise, God had other ideas. First they were shown the relationship between faith as a divine gift and the development of holiness in practical life. And then, they received their mission: "God then thrust them out, utterly against their will, to raise a holy people," Wesley wrote. To fully understand the nuances of the Methodist movement over the subsequent fifty years of Wesley's life, we would have to go into a lot more detail. It's clear, though, that the message of holiness as a motivation underlay it all.

## Holiness and Discipleship

We tend to use the word "discipleship" much more than we use "holiness" today. This is somewhat understandable. Holiness can have some negative connotations in our own context. No one wants to be accused of being holier-than-thou, and everyone wants to avoid getting cornered by a holy roller! On the other hand, discipleship seems like a much more positive term. When we read about the life of Jesus, we find that his followers are called disciples. In the Great Commission at the end of the Gospel of Matthew, we see Jesus telling us to go into the world and make disciples of all nations. So discipleship is a thoroughgoing concept in the New Testament. What is interesting is that the term is practically missing in Wesley. If you consult the most authoritative index on Wesley's sermon corpus, you'll find exactly zero entries for "disciple" and "discipleship."

Why the disparity? Why would Wesley favor the language of holiness so thoroughly while ignoring terms related to discipleship? And why would we embrace discipleship language while allowing words related to holiness to ring negatively in our ears? The answers to those questions aren't entirely clear. It may help us to realize that holiness terms and discipleship terms tend to show up in different parts of the New Testament. It's in the Gospels that we find the disciples being described. These are—along with the Acts of the Apostles—the most narrative parts of the New Testament. Descriptions of holiness, on the other hand, are much more prominent in the letters of Paul, the letters of Peter, and the book of Hebrews. These books have much less of a narrative quality and much more a combination of theological description and moral counsel.

When it comes to Wesley, the prominence of terms related to *holiness* and *sanctification* ironically tells us something about how he understands *discipleship* (in concept if not in the word itself). Holiness isn't just a conformity to an outward standard of life. Such behavior might be nothing more than a kind of hollow moralism. Instead, holiness is about what it means to be transformed *inwardly* by God's grace so that the *outward* life is changed as a result. It isn't that Wesley ignores the narratives of the Gospels and the early church in Acts. Far from it. But it is perhaps accurate to say that, when he wants to describe what the life of true faith looks like, he often accentuates portions of the New Testament that favor holiness language exactly because they point to the necessity of the inward change. So if we want to understand the Wesleyan vision of discipleship, we have to see it as a dynamic and transformative kind of life whereby we live differently because we are becoming different persons through the power of God's grace.

## The Sermon Content of this Volume

This volume contains a set of nine sermons written at different times in John Wesley's life that all seek to describe what we would call true discipleship. His abiding concern in practically all his published sermons is to encourage his audience to learn what it means to be an "altogether Christian" (to use his phrase from *The Almost Christian*). In Wesley's understanding, this isn't something that any of us can do alone. In one sense, we can't do it by ourselves because the only true holiness is social holiness—by which he means the holiness that can develop within us when we are deeply rooted in a community of fellow believers. Even more importantly, Wesley doesn't think we could become alto-gether Christians without the distinct witness of the Holy Spirit in our lives enabling us to have true faith in Christ and to live our lives in response to that faith.

Living as an authentic disciple of Jesus Christ, in other words, requires the ongoing gift of God's grace. In *The Good Steward*, Wesley describes what that looks like with reference to our stewardship of all that God has entrusted us with:

> It is no small thing to lay out for God all which you have received from God. It requires all your wisdom, all your resolution, all your patience, and constancy; —far more than ever you had by nature; but not more than you may have by grace. For his grace is sufficient for you; and "all things," you know, "are possible to him that believeth." By faith, then, "put on the Lord Jesus Christ;" "put on the whole armour of God"; and you shall be enabled to glorify him in all your words and works; yea, to bring every thought into captivity to the obedience of Christ!

Wesley would say that the one who is living such a life is living a holy life. We might say that such a person is an authentic disciple of Jesus Christ. Regardless of the term preferred, it's clear that grace and a grace-enabled faith are the prerequisites.

A few notes are in order to help the reader understand why the sermons in this volume have been chosen and how the collection has been arranged. Over half a century separates the sermon written earliest (*Circumcision of the Heart*, 1733) from the one written latest (*The More Excellent Way*, 1787). While the sermons have been arranged chrono-logically from earliest to latest in this volume, that decision was not made for chronological reasons alone. Rather, this arrangement of the sermons also communicates something important about the character of present salvation in John Wesley's view. *Circumcision of the Heart*, our first entry, offers an expansive vision of the Christian life as encompassing humility, faith, hope, and love. Then the four sermons that follow build upon this theme, though with a level of evangelical zeal and expectation that can almost take one's breath away. These include *The Almost Christian*, *The First-Fruits of the Spirit*, *The Way to the Kingdom*, and *Marks of the New Birth*. (Wesley's tutelage to the Moravians and experience at Aldersgate occurred between his writing of *Circumcision of the Heart* and the writing of these next four, which is significant for the tone of the latter.)

The next three sermons tend to moderate those that precede them just a bit. They offer a pastoral perspective on Christian discipleship that emphasizes the need for grace to continue the sanctifying work begun when a believer is justified and experiences new birth. *On Sin in Believers* and *The Repentance of Believers* deal with the reality of sin's presence in the lives of Christian believers. Yet these two sermons also make a case that the lingering presence of sin can be utterly defeated by grace. *The Good Steward* looks at the issue of stewardship on multiple levels: from the stewardship of material goods, to the stewardship of one's time and activities, to the stewardship of both body and soul, and finally to the stewardship of God's grace. It offers the reader a compelling argument for the life that is possible when God's grace becomes the driving force in it. There is a pastoral quality to these three sermons that makes them an important component of the Wesleyan vision of discipleship.

Finally, we conclude with *The More Excellent Way*. This is a sermon written very late in Wesley's life. In it he seems to have come to the conclusion that there will always be "two orders" of Christians: those who settle for a faith that is barely sufficient, and those who desire to fully embrace the more excellent way of holy love. The sermon is a fitting capstone to the collection; it is pastorally generous to disciples who are at many points along their journey, but in true Wesleyan fashion it also contains the evangelical encouragement to pursue the holy life every day and so aim for the "summit of Christian holiness." Taken together, all nine sermons offer a broad view of John Wesley's understanding of discipleship. They present a view of the Christian life relevant for any age.

## Notes on Format and Editorial Considerations

The Wesley sermon material used in the John Wesley Collection is drawn from the nineteenth-century edition of Wesley's works prepared by Thomas Jackson. Where necessary, the Jackson edition sermon texts have been compared to eighteenth-century first editions either from the relevant volume of Wesley's *Sermons on Several Occasions* or from sermons published singly. By collecting small groups of sermons together under particular topics (such as discipleship), our hope is that the vital Wesleyan theology contained in these sermons will reach a broad audience. Since we have made some editorial decisions regarding the form and presentation of the sermons that mark a departure from the Jackson edition, a few notes on those changes are in order here.

The most immediately noticeable editorial change made in this volume is the insertion of section headings throughout each of Wesley's sermons. Our decision to insert these headings (and subheadings) has been made for the same reason that publishers of study Bibles insert section headings within the books of the Bible. The headings serve as an aid to the reader, so that the particular topic being dealt with in that part of the text is clear.

Another less noticeable editorial change has been to make slight modifications to the language of the sermons at certain points to make them more easily readable for a contemporary audience. These changes are few in number and represent a highly selective practice of changing only the most difficult to understand words or phrases. Sometimes that comes in the form of Scripture quotations, and in those instances our practice has been to "blend" the Authorized (or King James) Version that Wesley used with the New King James Version (which keeps the rhythms of the original KJV but includes some modernized language). At other times, we have changed words that come from Wesley's own pen—whether his original words or his own paraphrase of Scripture—again, in a way that preserves meaning but increases readability. Since our addition is not intended to be for scholarly use but rather for spiritual reading by a broad audience, we have not emphasized these changes with copious footnotes. We have, however, followed a two-fold set of criteria that can be summarized as: 1) Changes in language made as sparingly as possible and always to those passages in Wesley that seem to be the most obscure to the contemporary reader; 2) Substitutions in a word or a phrase always made with a concern for hewing as close to Wesley's meaning as possible.

A final note can be offered to explain the system of numbered paragraphs that are a feature of all Wesley's sermons. With only a few exceptions, Wesley's practice is to arrange his sermons so that each major section of the sermon is given a Roman numeral (I, II, III) while the paragraphs within each major section are given Arabic numerals (1, 2, 3). That system is retained in the Jackson edition of

Wesley's works, and we have kept it here as well. Our insertion of descriptive section headings typically corresponds to Wesley's Roman numeral divisions—in other words, we are simply elaborating on a system that he himself originally put in place. In addition, we have included subheadings within major sections at appropriate points as an aide to the reader. The one exception to how we've handled Wesley's numbering system has to do with the sermon *The Almost Christian*. In the original edition of that sermon, Wesley employs a paragraph numbering system more complicated than his norm which involves a second set of Roman numerals alongside his typical first set that denote different sections of the sermon. Arabic numerals are also used. When reading the sermon, this means that there is a third set of numbers to deal with, and the effect is more confusing than clarifying for the reader. We made the decision to remove the third set of numbers, which we believe both brings the sermon into greater conformity with Wesley's general practice and serves to benefit the general reader.

Andrew C. Thompson
Executive Editor

*From*

| A | L | M | O | S | T |

*to*

| ALTOGETHER |

# ONE

# The Circumcision of the Heart

## 1733

*Circumcision is that of the heart, in the spirit, and not in the letter.*

—Romans 2:29

## Introduction

1. It is the melancholy remark of an excellent man, that he who now preaches the most essential duties of Christianity, runs the hazard of being esteemed, by a great part of his hearers, "a setter forth of new doctrines." Most men have so *lived away* the substance of that religion, the profession of which they still retain, that no sooner are any of those truths proposed which difference the Spirit of Christ from the spirit of the world, than they cry out, "You bring strange things to our ears; we would know what these things mean": though he is only preaching to them "Jesus and the

resurrection," with the necessary consequence of it, if Christ be risen, you ought then to die unto the world, and to live wholly unto God.

2. This is a hard saying to the natural man, who is alive unto the world, and dead unto God; and one that he will not readily be persuaded to receive as the truth of God, unless it be so qualified in the interpretation, as to have neither use nor significance left. He "receives not the" words "of the Spirit of God," taken in their plain and obvious meaning; "they are foolishness unto him; neither" indeed "can he know them, because they are spiritually discerned." They are perceivable only by that spiritual sense, which in him was never yet awakened for want of which he must reject, as idle fancies of men, what are both the wisdom and the power of God.

3. That "circumcision is that of the heart, in the spirit, and not in the letter"—that the distinguishing mark of a true follower of Christ, of one who is in a state of acceptance with God, is not either outward circumcision, or baptism, or any other outward form, but a right state of soul, a mind and spirit renewed after the image of him that created it—is one of those important truths that can only be spiritually discerned. And this the Apostle himself intimates in the next words, "Whose praise is not of men, but of God." As if he had said, "Do not expect, whoever you are, who thus follows your great Master, that the world, the one who follow him not, will say, 'Well done, good and faithful servant!' Know that the circumcision of the heart, the seal of your calling, is foolishness with the world. Be content to wait for your applause till the day of your Lord's appearing. In that day shalt you have praise of God, in the great assembly of men and angels."

I design, first, particularly to inquire of what this circumcision of the heart consists; and, secondly, to mention some reflections that naturally arise from such an inquiry.

# I. What Circumcision of the Heart Implies

1. I am, first, to inquire, of what that circumcision of the heart consists, which will receive the praise of God. In general we may observe, it is that habitual disposition of soul which, in the sacred writings, is termed holiness; and which directly implies, the being cleansed from sin, "from all filthiness both of flesh and spirit," and, by consequence, the being endued with those virtues which were also in Christ Jesus; the being so "renewed in the spirit of our mind," as to be "perfect as our Father in heaven is perfect."

## Circumcision of the Heart Implies a Deep Humility

2. To be more particular: circumcision of heart implies humility, faith, hope, and charity. Humility, a right judgment of ourselves, cleanses our minds from those high conceits of our own perfection, from that undue opinion of our own abilities and attainments, which are the genuine fruit of a corrupted nature. This entirely cuts off that vain thought, "I am rich, and wise, and have need of nothing," and convinces us that we are by nature wretched, and poor, and miserable, and blind, and naked. It convinces us, that in our best estate we are, of ourselves, all sin and vanity; that confusion, and ignorance, and error reign over our understanding; that unreasonable, earthly, sensual, devilish passions usurp authority over our will; in a word, that there is no whole part in our soul, that all the foundations of our nature are out of course.

3. At the same time we are convinced, that we are not sufficient of ourselves to help ourselves; that, without the Spirit of God, we can do nothing but add sin to sin; that it is he alone who works in us by his almighty power, either to will or do that which is good; it being as impossible for us even to think a good thought, without the supernatural assistance of his Spirit, as to create ourselves, or to renew our whole souls in righteousness and true holiness.

4. A sure effect of our having formed this right judgment of the sinfulness and helplessness of our nature is a disregard of that "honor which comes of man," which is usually paid to some supposed excellency in us. He who knows himself, neither desires nor values the applause that he knows he does not deserve. It is therefore "a very small thing with him, to be judged by man's judgment." He has all reason to think, by comparing what it has said, either for or against him, with what he feels in his own breast, that the world, as well as the god of this world, was "a liar from the beginning." And even as to those who are not of the world; though he would choose, if it were the will of God, that they should account of him as of one desirous to be found a faithful steward of his Lord's goods, if by chance this might be a means of enabling him to be of more use to his fellow-servants, yet as this is the one end of his wishing for their approbation, so he does not at all rest upon it. For he is assured, that whatever God wills, he can never lack instruments to perform; since he is able, even of these stones, to raise up servants to do his pleasure.

## Circumcision of the Heart Implies a Steadfast Faith

5. This is that lowliness of mind, which they have learned of Christ, who follow his example and tread in

his steps. And this knowledge of their disease, whereby they are more and more cleansed from one part of it, pride and vanity, disposes them to embrace, with a willing mind, the second thing implied in circumcision of the heart—that faith which alone is able to make them whole, which is the one medicine given under heaven to heal their sickness.

6. The best guide of the blind, the surest light of them that are in darkness, the most perfect instructor of the foolish, is faith. But it must be such a faith as is "mighty through God, to the pulling down of strongholds," to the overturning of all the prejudices of corrupt reason, all the false maxims revered among men, all evil customs and habits, all that "wisdom of the world which is foolishness with God"; as "casts down imaginations," reasoning, "and every high thing that exalts itself against the knowledge of God, and brings into captivity every thought to the obedience of Christ."

7. "All things are possible to him who" thus "believes." "The eyes of his understanding being enlightened," he sees what is his calling—even to glorify God, who has bought him with so high a price, in his body and in his spirit, which now are God's by redemption, as well as by creation. He feels what is "the exceeding greatness of this power," who, as he raised up Christ from the dead, so is able to revive us, dead in sin, "by his Spirit which dwells in us."

"This is the victory which overcomes the world, even our faith"; that faith, which is not only an unshaken assent to all that God has revealed in Scripture—and in particular to those important truths: "Jesus Christ came into the world to save sinners"; "he bore our sins in his own body on the tree"; "he is the propitiation for our sins, and not for ours only, but also for the sins of the whole world"*—but likewise the revelation of Christ in our hearts; a divine evidence or conviction of his love, his free, unmerited love to me a sinner; a sure confidence in his pardoning mercy, wrought in us by the Holy Spirit; a confidence, by which every true believer is enabled to bear witness: "I know that my Redeemer lives," that I have an "Advocate with the Father," and that "Jesus Christ the righteous" is my Lord, and "the propitiation for my sins"; I know he has "loved me, and given himself for me"; he has reconciled me, even me, to God; and I "have redemption through his blood, even the forgiveness of sins."

8. Such a faith as this cannot fail to show evidently the power of him that inspires it, by delivering his children from the yoke of sin, and "purging their consciences from dead works"; by strengthening them so that they are no longer constrained to obey sin in the desires thereof; but instead of yielding their members unto it, as "instruments of unrighteousness," they now "yield themselves" entirely "unto God, as those that are alive from the dead."

## *Circumcision of the Heart Implies a Lively Hope*

9. Those who are thus by faith born of God, have also strong consolation through hope. This is the next thing that the circumcision of the heart implies; even the testimony of their own spirit with the Spirit which witnesses in their hearts that they are the children of God. Indeed it is the same

---

*Wesley originally included a parenthetical note in the body of the sermon at this point that reads, "The following part of this paragraph is now added to the sermon formerly preached." He is pointing to a difference between the original version of Circumcision of the Heart in 1733 and the version he published in 1748. The added lines are meant to strengthen the evangelical character of faith as a

Spirit who works in them that clear and cheerful confidence that their heart is upright toward God; that good assurance, that they now do, through his grace, the things which are acceptable in his sight; that they are now in the path which leads to life, and shall, by the mercy of God, endure in it to the end. It is he who gives them a lively expectation of receiving all good things at God's hand; a joyous prospect of that crown of glory, which is reserved in heaven for them.

By this anchor a Christian is kept steady in the midst of the waves of this troublesome world, and preserved from striking upon either of those fatal rocks—presumption or despair. He is neither discouraged by the misconceived severity of his Lord, nor does he "despise the riches of his goodness." He neither apprehends the difficulties of the race set before him to be greater than he has strength to conquer, nor expects there to be so little as to yield in the conquest, till he has put forth all strength. The experience he already has in the Christian warfare, as it assures him his "labor is not in vain," if "whatever he finds to do, he does it with his might"; so it forbids his entertaining so vain a thought, as that he can otherwise gain any advantage, as that any virtue can be shown, any praise attained, by faint hearts and feeble hands; or, indeed, by any but those who pursue the same course with the great Apostle of the Gentiles—"I," says he, "so run, not as uncertainly; I so fight, not as one who beats the air: but I keep under my body, and bring it into subjection; lest, by

---

personal assurance of Christ's love in the heart of the believer—in other words, not just that Christ died for the sins of the whole but that Christ also died for *me*. The parenthetical is removed in this edition both because it breaks up the text and because of Wesley's use of the archaic abbreviation "N.B." (or "nota bene") which would only confuse the contemporary reader.

any means, when I have preached to others, I myself should be a castaway."

10. By the same discipline is every good soldier of Christ to inure himself to endure hardship. Confirmed and strengthened by this, he will be able not only to renounce the works of darkness, but every appetite too, and every affection, which is not subject to the law of God. For "every one," says St. John, "who has this hope, purifies himself even as he is pure." It is his daily care, by the grace of God in Christ, and through the blood of the covenant, to purge the inmost recesses of his soul from the lusts that before possessed and defiled it; from uncleanness, and envy, and malice, and wrath; from every passion and temper that is after the flesh, that either springs from or cherishes his native corruption; as well knowing, that he whose very body is the temple of God, ought to admit into it nothing common or unclean; and that holiness becomes that house for ever, where the Spirit of holiness vouchsafes to dwell.

## Circumcision of the Heart Implies Love

11. Yet you lack one thing, whosoever you are, that to a deep humility, and a steadfast faith, has joined a lively hope, and thereby in a good measure cleansed your heart from its inbred pollution. If you will be perfect, add to all these, charity; add love, and you have the circumcision of the heart. "Love is the fulfilling of the law, the end of the commandment." Very excellent things are spoken of love; it is the essence, the spirit, the life of all virtue. It is not only the first and great command, but it is all the commandments in one. "Whatsoever things are just, whatsoever things are pure, whatsoever things are amiable," or honorable; "if there be any virtue, if there be any praise," they are all comprised

in this one word—love. In this is perfection, and glory, and happiness. The royal law of heaven and earth is this, "You shall love the Lord your God with all your heart, and with all your soul, and with all your mind, and with all your strength."

12. Not that this forbids us to love anything besides God: it implies that we love our brother also. Nor yet does it forbid us (as some have strangely imagined) to take pleasure in any thing but God. To suppose this, is to suppose the Fountain of holiness is directly the author of sin; since he has inseparably annexed pleasure to the use of those creatures that are necessary to sustain the life he has given us. This, therefore, can never be the meaning of his command. What the real sense of it is, both our blessed Lord and his Apostles tell us too frequently, and too plainly, to be misunderstood. They all with one mouth bear witness, that the true meaning of those several declarations, "The Lord your God is one Lord"; "You shall have no other Gods but me"; "You shall love the Lord your God with all your strength"; "You shall cleave unto him"; "The desire of your soul shall be to his name"; is no other than this: the one perfect Good shall be your one ultimate end.

One thing shall you desire for its own sake—the fruition of him that is All in All. One happiness shall you propose to your souls, even a union with him that made them; the having "fellowship with the Father and the Son"; the being joined to the Lord in one Spirit. One design you are to pursue to the end of time—the enjoyment of God in time and in eternity. Desire other things, so far as they tend to this. Love the creature as it leads to the Creator. But in every step you take, be this the glorious point that terminates your view. Let every affection, and thought, and word, and work, be subordinate to this. Whatever you desire or fear, whatever you seek or shun, whatever you think, speak, or do, be it in order to your happiness in God, the sole End, as well as Source, of your being.

13. Have no end, no ultimate end, but God. Thus our Lord: "One thing is needful." And if your eye be singly fixed on this one thing, "your whole body shall be full of light." Thus St. Paul: "This one thing I do; I press toward the mark, for the prize of the high calling in Christ Jesus." Thus St. James: "Cleanse your hands, you sinners, and purify your hearts, you double-minded." Thus St. John: "Love not the world, neither the things that are in the world. For all that is in the world, the lust of the flesh, the lust of the eye, and the pride of life, is not of the Father, but is of the world." The seeking happiness in what gratifies either the desire of the flesh, by agreeably striking upon the outward senses; the desire of the eye, of the imagination, by its novelty, greatness, or beauty; or the pride of life, whether by pomp, grandeur, power, or, the usual consequence of them, applause and admiration; "is not of the Father," comes not from, neither is approved by, the Father of spirits; "but of the world": it is the distinguishing mark of those who will not have him to reign over them.

## II. Reflections on Circumcision of the Heart

*No One Shall Claim the Praise of God, unless His Heart Is Circumcised by Humility*

1. I have thus particularly inquired, what that circumcision of heart is, which will obtain the praise of God. I am, in the second place, to mention some reflections that naturally arise from such an inquiry, as a plain rule by which every man may judge of himself, whether he is of the world or of God. And, first, it is clear from what has been said, that

no man has a title to the praise of God, unless his heart is circumcised by humility; unless he is little, and base, and vile in his own eyes; unless he is deeply convinced of that inbred "corruption of his nature," "by which he is very far gone from original righteousness," being prone to all evil, averse to all good, corrupt and abominable; having a "carnal mind which is enmity against God, and is not subject to the law of God, nor indeed can be," unless he continually feels in his inmost soul, that without the Spirit of God resting upon him, he can neither think, nor desire, nor speak, nor act anything good, or well-pleasing in his sight. No man I say, has a title to the praise of God, till he feels his want of God; nor indeed, till he seeks that "honor which comes of God only"; and neither desires nor pursues that which comes of man, unless so far only as it tends to this.

## No One Shall Claim the Honor of God, unless His Heart Is Circumcised by Faith

2. Another truth, which naturally follows from what has been said, is, that none shall obtain the honor that comes from God, unless his heart be circumcised by faith; even a "faith of the operation of God"; unless, refusing to be any longer led by his senses, appetites, or passions, or even by that blind leader of the blind, so idolized by the world, natural reason, he lives and walks by faith. He directs every step, as "seeking him that is invisible"; "looks not at the things that are seen, which are temporal, but at the things that are not seen, which are eternal"; and governs all his desires, designs, and thoughts, all his actions and conversations, as one who has entered in within the veil, where Jesus sits at the right hand of God.

3. It were to be wished, that they were better acquainted with this faith, who employ much of their time and pains

in laying another foundation; in grounding religion on the eternal *fitness* of things on the intrinsic *excellence* of virtue, and the *beauty* of actions flowing from it; on the *reasons* as they term them, of good and evil, and the *relations* of beings to each other. Either these accounts of the grounds of Christian duty coincide with the scriptural, or not. If they do, why are well-meaning men perplexed, and drawn from the weightier matters of the law, by a cloud of terms, by which the easiest truths are explained into obscurity? If they are not, then it behooves them to consider who is the author of this new doctrine; whether he is likely to be an angel from heaven, who preaches another gospel than that of Christ Jesus; though, if he were, God, not we, has pronounced his sentence: "Let him be accursed."

4. Our gospel, as it knows no other foundation of good works than faith, or of faith than Christ, so it clearly informs us: we are not his disciples while we either deny him to be the Author, or his Spirit to be the Inspirer and Perfecter, both of our faith and works. "If any man does not have the spirit of Christ, he is not his." He alone can revive those who are dead unto God, can breathe into them the breath of Christian life, and so prevent, accompany, and follow them with his grace, as to bring their good desires to good effect. And, "as many as are thus led by the Spirit of God, they are the sons of God." This is God's short and plain account of true religion and virtue, and "no other foundation can any man lay."

## No One Shall Claim the Crown of God, unless His Heart Is Circumcised by Hope

5. From what has been said, we may, thirdly, learn that none is truly "led by the Spirit," unless that "Spirit bear witness with his spirit, that he is a child of God"; unless he see the

prize and the crown before him, and "rejoice in hope of the glory of God." So greatly have they erred who have taught that, in serving God, we ought not to have a view to our own happiness! More than that, we are often and expressly taught of God, to have "respect unto the compensation of reward"; to balance toil with the "joy set before us," these "light afflictions" with that "exceeding weight of glory." Indeed, we are "aliens to the covenant of promise," we are "without God in the world," until God, "according to his great mercy, he has caused us to be born again to a living hope through the resurrection of Jesus Christ from the dead, to an inheritance that is imperishable, undefiled, and unfading" (ESV).

6. But if these things are so, it is high time for those persons to deal faithfully with their own souls who are so far from finding in themselves this joyful assurance that they fulfill the terms, and shall obtain the promises, of that covenant, as to quarrel with the covenant itself, and blaspheme the terms of it; to complain, they are too severe; and that no man ever did or shall live up to them. What is this but to reproach God, as if he were a hard master, requiring of his servants more than he enables them to perform—as if he had mocked the helpless works of his hands, by binding them to impossibilities; by commanding them to overcome, where neither their own strength nor grace was sufficient for them?

7. These blasphemers might almost persuade those to imagine themselves guiltless, who, in the contrary extreme, hope to fulfill the commands of God, without taking any pains at all. Vain hope! That a child of Adam should ever expect to see the kingdom of Christ and of God, without striving, without *agonizing*, first "to enter in at the narrow gate"—that one who, as "conceived and born in sin," and whose "inward parts are very wickedness," should once entertain a thought of being "purified as his Lord is pure,"

unless he tread in his steps, and "take up his cross daily"; unless he "cut off his right hand," and "pluck out the right eye, and cast it from him"—that he should ever dream of shaking off his old opinions, passions, tempers, of being "sanctified throughout in spirit, soul, and body," without a constant and continued course of general self-denial!

8. What less than this can we possibly infer from the above-cited words of St. Paul, who, living "in infirmities, in reproaches, in necessities, in persecutions, in distresses" for Christ's sake; who, being full of "signs, and wonders, and mighty deeds"; who, having been "caught up into the third heaven"; yet reckoned, as a late author strongly expresses it, that all his virtues would be insecure, and even his salvation in danger, without this constant self-denial? "So I run," says he, "not with uncertainty; so I fight, not as one who beats the air," by which he plainly teaches us, that he who does not thus run, who does not thus deny himself daily, does run with uncertainty, and fights to as little purpose as he that "beats the air."

## No One Shall Claim the Glory of God, unless His Heart Is Circumcised by Love

9. To as little purpose does he talk of "fighting the fight of faith," as vainly hope to attain the crown of incorruption (as we may, lastly, infer from the preceding observations), whose heart is not circumcised by love. Love, cutting off both the lust of the flesh, the lust of the eye, and the pride of life—engaging the whole man, body, soul, and spirit, in the ardent pursuit of that one object—is so essential to a child of God, that, without it, whosoever lives is counted dead before him. "Though I speak with the tongues of men and of angels, and have not love, I am as sounding brass, or a tinkling cymbal. Though I have the gift of prophecy, and

understand all mysteries, and all knowledge; and though I have all faith, so as to remove mountains, and have not love, I am nothing." Indeed, "though I give all my goods to feed the poor, and my body to be burned, and have not love, it profits me nothing."

10. Here, then, is the sum of the perfect law; this is the true circumcision of the heart. Let the spirit return to God that gave it, with the whole train of its affections. "Unto the place from which all the rivers came" to that place, let them flow again. Other sacrifices from us he would not; but the living sacrifice of the heart he has chosen. Let it be continually offered up to God through Christ, in flames of holy love. And let no creature be suffered to share with him: for he is a jealous God. He will not divide his throne with another; he will reign without a rival. Be no design, no desire admitted there, but whatever has him for its ultimate object. This is the way in which those children of God once walked, who, being dead, still speak to us: "Desire not to live, but to praise his name. Let all your thoughts, words, and works, tend to his glory. Set your heart firm on him, and on other things only as they are in and from him. Let your soul be filled with so entire a love of him, that you may love nothing but for his sake."

"Have a pure intention of heart, a steadfast regard to his glory in all your actions." "Fix your eye upon the blessed hope of your calling, and make all the things of the world minister unto it." For then, and not till then is that "mind in us which was also in Christ Jesus"; when, in every motion of our heart, in every word of our tongue, in every work of our hands, we "pursue nothing but in relation to him, and in subordination to his pleasure"; when we, too, neither think, nor speak, nor act, to fulfill our "own will, but the will of him that sent us"; when, "whether we eat, or drink, or whatever we do, we do all to the glory of God."

# TWO

# THE ALMOST CHRISTIAN

## 1741

*"You almost persuade me to become a Christian."*
—Acts 26:28 NKJV

## Introduction

And many there are who go thus far: ever since the Christian religion was in the world, there have been many in every age and nation who were almost persuaded to be Christians. But seeing it avails nothing before God to go *only thus far*, it highly concerns us to consider, first, what is implied in being *almost*, and secondly, what in being *altogether, a Christian*.

## I. What Is Implied in Being *Almost* a Christian?

### *Heathen Honesty*

1. Now, in the being *almost a Christian* is implied, first, heathen honesty. No one, I suppose, will make any question

of this; especially, since by heathen honesty here, I mean, not that which is recommended in the writings of their philosophers only, but such as the common heathens expected one of another, and many of them actually practiced. By the rules of this they were taught that they ought not to be unjust; not to take away their neighbor's goods, either by robbery or theft; not to oppress the poor, neither to use extortion toward any; not to cheat or overreach either the poor or rich, in whatsoever commerce they had with them; to defraud no man of his right; and, if it were possible, to owe no man anything.

2. Again, the common heathens allowed that some regard was to be paid to truth, as well as to justice. And, accordingly, they not only held him in abomination who was forsworn, who called God to witness to a lie; but he also who was known to be a slanderer of his neighbor, who falsely accused any man. And indeed, little better did they esteem willful liars of any sort, accounting them the disgrace of humankind and the pests of society.

3. Yet again, there was a sort of love and assistance which they expected one from another. They expected whatever assistance any one could give another, without prejudice to himself. And this they extended not only to those little offices of humanity which are performed without any expense or labor, but likewise to the feeding the hungry, if they had food to spare; the clothing the naked with their own superfluous raiment; and, in general, the giving, to any that needed, such things as they needed not themselves. Thus far, in the lowest account of it, heathen honesty went; the first thing implied in the being *almost a Christian.*

## The Form of Godliness

4. A second thing implied in the being *almost a Christian* is, the having a form of godliness; of that godliness which

is prescribed in the gospel of Christ; the having the *outside of a real Christian*. Accordingly, the almost Christian does nothing that the gospel forbids. He takes not the name of God in vain; he blesses, and curses not; he swears not at all, but his communication is, yes, yes; no, no. He profanes not the day of the Lord, nor suffers it to be profaned, even by the stranger that is within his gates. He not only avoids all actual adultery, fornication, and uncleanness, but every word or look that either directly or indirectly tends thereto; indeed, all idle words, abstaining both from detraction, backbiting, gossiping, evil speaking, and from εὐτραπελία, *all foolish talking and jesting*—a kind of virtue in the heathen moralist's account—briefly, from all conversation that is not "good to the use of edifying," and that, consequently, "grieves the Holy Spirit of God, whereby we are sealed to the day of redemption."

5. He abstains from "wine in which is excess"; from reveling and gluttony. He avoids, as much as in him lies, all strife and contention, continually endeavoring to live peaceably with all men. And, if he suffers wrong, he avenges not himself, neither returns evil for evil. He is no mocker, no brawler, no scoffer, either at the faults or infirmities of his neighbor. He does not willingly wrong, hurt, or grieve any man; but in all things acts and speaks by that plain rule, "Whatever you would not want one to do unto you, that do not to another."

6. And in doing good, he does not confine himself to cheap and easy offices of kindness, but labors and suffers for the profit of many, that by all means he may help some. In spite of toil or pain, "whatsoever his hand finds to do, he does it with his might"; whether it be for his friends, or for his enemies; for the evil, or for the good. For being "not slothful" in this, or in any "business," as he "has opportunity" he does

"good," all manner of good, "to all men," and to their souls as well as their bodies. He reproves the wicked, instructs the ignorant, confirms the wavering, quickens the good, and comforts the afflicted. He labors to awaken those that sleep; to lead those whom God has already awakened to the "fountain opened for sin and for uncleanness," that they may wash in it and be clean; and to stir up those who are saved through faith, to adorn the gospel of Christ in all things.

7. He that has the form of godliness uses also the means of grace; indeed, all of them, and at all opportunities. He constantly frequents the house of God; and that, not as the manner of some is, who come into the presence of the Most High, either loaded with gold and costly apparel, or in all the gaudy vanity of dress, and either by their unseasonable civilities to each other, or the impertinent gaiety of their behavior, disclaim all pretensions to the form as well as to the power of godliness.

Would to God there were none even among ourselves who fall under the same condemnation! Who come into this house, it may be, gazing about, or with all the signs of the most listless, careless indifference, though sometimes they may *seem* to use a prayer to God for his blessing on what they are entering upon; who, during that awful service, are either asleep, or reclined in the most convenient posture for it; or, as though they supposed God were asleep, talking with one another, or looking round, as utterly void of employment. Neither let these be accused of the form of godliness. No, he who has even this, behaves with seriousness and attention, in every part of that solemn service. More especially, when he approaches the table of the Lord, it is not with a light or careless behavior, but with an air, gesture, and deportment that speaks nothing else but "God be merciful to me a sinner!"

8. To this, if we add the constant use of family prayer, by those who are masters of families, and the setting times apart for private addresses to God, with a daily seriousness of behavior; he who uniformly practices this outward religion, has the form of godliness. There needs but one thing more in order to his being *almost a Christian*, and that is, sincerity.

## Sincerity

9. By sincerity I mean, a real, inward principle of religion, from which these outward actions flow. And, indeed if we have not this, we have not heathen honesty; no, not so much of it as will answer the demand of a heathen Epicurean poet. Even this poor wretch, in his sober intervals, is able to testify,

> *Oderunt peccare boni, virtutis amore;*
> *Oderunt peccare mali, formidine poenae.*
> [Good men avoid sin from the love of virtue;
> Wicked men avoid sin from a fear of punishment.]

So that, if a man only abstains from doing evil in order to avoid punishment, *non pasces in cruce corvos*, (you shall not be hanged), says the Pagan; there, "you have your reward." But even he will not allow such a harmless man as this to be so much as a *good heathen*. If, then, any man, from the same motive, namely, to avoid punishment, to avoid the loss of his friends, or his gain, or his reputation, should not only abstain from doing evil, but also do ever so much good; indeed, and use all the means of grace; yet we could not with any propriety say, this man is even *almost a Christian*. If he has no better principle in his heart, he is only a hypocrite altogether.

10. Sincerity, therefore, is necessarily implied in the being *almost a Christian*; a real design to serve God, a hearty desire to do his will. It is necessarily implied, that a man have

a sincere view of pleasing God in all things; in all his conversation, in all his actions, in all he does or leaves undone. This design, if any man is *almost a Christian*, runs through the whole tenor of his life. This is the moving principle, both in his doing good, his abstaining from evil, and his using the ordinances of God.

## Wesley's Testimony

11. But here it will probably be inquired, "Is it possible that any man living should go so far as this, and, nevertheless, be *only almost a Christian*? What more than this, can be implied in the being *a Christian altogether*? I answer, first, that it is possible to go thus far, and yet be but *almost a Christian*. I learn, not only from the oracles of God, but also from the sure testimony of experience.

12. Brethren, great is "my boldness towards you in this behalf." And "forgive me this wrong," if I declare my own folly upon the housetop, for yours and the gospel's sake. Suffer me, then, to speak freely of myself, even as of another man. I am content to be abased, so you may be exalted, and to be yet viler for the glory of my Lord.

13. I did go thus far for many years, as many of this place can testify; using diligence to eschew all evil, and to have a conscience void of offense; redeeming the time; buying up every opportunity of doing all good to all men; constantly and carefully using all the public and all the private means of grace; endeavoring after a steady seriousness of behavior, at all times, and in all places; and, God is my record, before whom I stand, doing all this in sincerity; having a real design to serve God; a hearty desire to do his will in all things; to please him who had called me to "fight the good fight," and to "lay hold of eternal life." Yet my own conscience bears me

witness in the Holy Ghost that all this time I was but *almost a Christian*.

## II. What Is Implied in Being *Altogether a Christian*?

### *The Love of God*

1. If it is inquired, "What more than this is implied in the being *altogether a Christian*?" I answer first, the love of God. For thus says his word, "You shall love the Lord your God with all your heart, and with all your soul, and with all your mind, and with all your strength." Such a love is this, as engrosses the whole heart, as rakes up all the affections, as fills the entire capacity of the soul and employs the utmost extent of all its faculties. He that thus loves the Lord his God, his spirit continually "rejoices in God his Savior." His delight is in the Lord, his Lord and his All, to whom "in everything he gives thanks. All his desire is unto God, and to the remembrance of his name."

His heart is ever crying out, "Whom have I in heaven but you? And there is none upon earth that I desire beside you." Indeed, what can he desire beside God? Not the world, or the things of the world: for he is "crucified to the world, and the world crucified to him." He is crucified to "the desire of the flesh, the desire of the eye, and the pride of life." Indeed, he is dead to pride of every kind: for "love is not puffed up" but "he that dwelling in love, dwells in God, and God in him," is less than nothing in his own eyes.

### *The Love of Our Neighbor*

2. The second thing implied in the being *altogether a Christian* is the love of our neighbor. For thus said our Lord

in the following words: "You shall love your neighbor as yourself." If any man should ask, "Who is my neighbor?" we reply: Every man in the world; every child of his who is the Father of the spirits of all flesh. Nor may we in any way exclude our enemies or the enemies of God and their own souls. But every Christian loves these also as himself, indeed, "as Christ loved us."

He that would more fully understand what manner of love this is, may consider St. Paul's description of it. It is "long-suffering and kind." It "envies not." It is not rash or hasty in judging. It "is not puffed up"; but makes him that loves, the least, the servant of all. Love "does not behave itself unseemly," but becomes "all things to all men." She "seeks not her own"; but only the good of others, that they may be saved. "Love is not provoked." It casts out wrath, which he who has is wanting in love. "It thinks no evil. It rejoices not in iniquity, but rejoices in the truth. It covers all things, believes all things, hopes all things, endures all things."

## Faith Working by Love

3. There is yet one thing more that may be separately considered, though it cannot actually be separate from the preceding, which is implied in the being *altogether a Christian*; and that is the ground of all, even faith. Very excellent things are spoken of this throughout the oracles of God. "Every one," says the beloved disciple, "who believes is born of God." "To as many as received him, he gave power to become the sons of God. Even to them who believe on his name." And "this is the victory that overcomes the world, even our faith." Indeed, our Lord himself declares, "He who believes in the Son has everlasting life; and comes not into condemnation, but is passed from death unto life."

4. But here let no man deceive his own soul. "It is diligently to be noted, the faith which does not bring forth repentance, and love, and all good works, is not that right living faith, but a dead and devilish one. For, even the devils believe that Christ was born of a virgin; that he wrought all kinds of miracles, declaring himself very God; that, for our sakes, he suffered a most painful death, to redeem us from death everlasting; that he rose again the third day; that he ascended into heaven, and sits at the right hand of the Father, and at the end of the world shall come again to judge both the living and dead. These articles of our faith the devils believe, and so they believe all that is written in the Old and New Testament. And yet for all this faith, they are but devils. They remain still in their damnable estate lacking the very true Christian faith."*

5. "The right and true Christian faith is" (to go on in the words of our own Church), "not only to believe that Holy Scripture and the Articles of our Faith are true, but also to have a sure trust and confidence to be saved from everlasting damnation by Christ. It is a sure trust and confidence which a man has in God, that, by the merits of Christ, his sins are forgiven, and he reconciled to the favor of God; by which does follow a loving heart, to obey his commandments."

6. Now, whosoever has this faith, which "purifies the heart" (by the power of God, who dwells in it) from "pride, anger, desire, from all unrighteousness," from "all filthiness of flesh and spirit"; which fills it with love stronger than death,

---

*The extended quotation in this paragraph is drawn from the "Homily on the Salvation of Man" from the first *Book of Homilies* of the Church of England. Wesley notes as much in the original edition of the sermon published in 1746.

both to God and to all mankind—love that does the works of God, glorying to spend and to be spent for all men, and that endures with joy, not only the reproach of Christ, the being mocked, despised, and hated of all men, but whatsoever the wisdom of God permits the malice of men or devils to inflict—whosoever has this faith thus working by love is not *almost* only, but *altogether*, a Christian.

## III. Is the Love of God Shed Abroad in Your Heart?

1. But who are the living witnesses of these things? I beseech you, brethren, as in the presence of that God before whom "hell and destruction are without a covering—how much more the hearts of the children of men?"—that each of you would ask his own heart, "Am I of that number? Do I so far practice justice, mercy, and truth, as even the rules of heathen honesty require? If so, have I the very *outside* of a Christian, the form of godliness? Do I abstain from evil—from whatsoever is forbidden in the written Word of God? Do I, whatever good my hand finds to do, do it with my might? Do I seriously use all the ordinances of God at all opportunities? And is all this done with a sincere design and desire to please God in all things?"

2. Are not many of you conscious, that you never came thus far; that you have not been even *almost a Christian*; that you have not come up to the standard of heathen honesty; at least, not to the form of Christian godliness; much less has God seen sincerity in you, a real design of pleasing him in all things? You never so much as intended to devote all your words and works, your business, studies, diversions, to his glory. You never even designed or desired, that whatsoever you did should be done "in the name of the Lord Jesus," and

as such should be "a spiritual sacrifice, acceptable to God through Christ."

3. But, supposing you had, do good designs and good desires make a Christian? By no means, unless they are brought to good effect. "Hell is paved," says one, "with good intentions." The great question of all, then, still remains. Is the love of God shed abroad in your heart? Can you cry out, "My God, and my All"? Do you desire nothing but him? Are you happy in God? Is he your glory, your delight, your crown of rejoicing? And is this commandment written in your heart, "That he who loves God must love his brother also" (NKJV)? Do you then love your neighbor as yourself? Do you love every man, even your enemies, even the enemies of God, as your own soul, as Christ loved you?

Indeed, do you believe that Christ loved you, and gave himself for you? Do you have faith in his blood? Do you believe the Lamb of God has taken away your sins, and cast them as a stone into the depth of the sea? That he has blotted out the handwriting that was against you, taking it out of the way, nailing it to his cross? Do you indeed have redemption through his blood, even the remission of your sins? And does his Spirit bear witness with your spirit, that you are a child of God?

4. The God and Father of our Lord Jesus Christ, who now stands in the midst of us, knows that if any man should die without this faith and this love, better it were for him that he had never been born. Awake, then, you who sleep, and call upon your God: call in the day when he may be found. Let him not rest, till he make his "goodness to pass before you"; till he proclaim unto you the name of the Lord: "The Lord, the Lord God, merciful and gracious, long-suffering, and abundant in goodness and truth, keeping mercy for thousands, forgiving iniquity, and transgression, and sin."

Let no man persuade you, by vain words, to rest short of this prize of your high calling. But cry unto him day and night, who, "while we were without strength, died for the ungodly," until you know in whom you have believed, and can say, "My Lord, and my God!" Remember, "always to pray, and not to faint," till you also can lift up your hand unto heaven, and declare to him who lives for ever and ever, "Lord, you know all things, you know that I love you."

5. May we all thus experience what it is to be, not *almost* only; but *altogether* Christians; being justified freely by his grace, through the redemption that is in Jesus; knowing we have peace with God through Jesus Christ; rejoicing in hope of the glory of God; and having the love of God shed abroad in our hearts, by the Holy Spirit given unto us!

# THREE

# THE FIRST-FRUITS OF THE SPIRIT

## 1746

*"There is therefore now no condemnation to those who are in Christ Jesus, who walk not after the flesh, but after the Spirit."*

—Romans 8:1

## Introduction

1. By "those who are in Christ Jesus," St. Paul evidently means those who truly believe in him; those who, "being justified by faith, have peace with God through our Lord Jesus Christ." They who thus believe do no longer "walk after the flesh," no longer follow the motions of corrupt nature, but "after the Spirit"; their thoughts, words, and works are under the direction of the blessed Spirit of God.

2. "There is therefore now no condemnation to" these. There is no condemnation to them from God; for he has

justified them "freely by his grace, through the redemption that is in Jesus." He has forgiven all their iniquities, and blotted out all their sins. And there is no condemnation to them from within; for they "have received, not the spirit of the world, but the Spirit which is of God; that they might know the things which are freely given to them of God" (1 Cor. 2:12); the Spirit which "bears witness with their spirits, that they are the children of God." And to this is added the testimony of their conscience, "that in simplicity and godly sincerity, not with fleshly wisdom, but by the grace of God, they have had their conversation in the world" (2 Cor. 1:12).

3. But because this Scripture has been so frequently misunderstood, and that in so dangerous a manner; because such multitudes of οἱ ἀμαθεῖς καὶ ἀστήρικτοι, *unlearned and unstable men*, men untaught of God, and consequently not established in the truth which is after godliness) have contorted it to their own destruction; I propose to show, as clearly as I can, first, who they are "who are in Christ Jesus," and "walk not after the flesh, but after the Spirit"; and, secondly, how "there is no condemnation to" these. I shall conclude with some practical inferences.

## I. Who Are They That "Are in Christ Jesus"?

1. First, I am to show who they are that "are in Christ Jesus." And are they not those who believe in his name—those who are "found in him, not having their own righteousness, but the righteousness which is of God by faith"? These, "who have redemption through his blood," are properly said to be in him; for they dwell in Christ, and Christ in them. They are joined unto the Lord in one Spirit. They are grafted into him as branches into the vine. They are united, as members

to their head, in a manner that words cannot express, nor could it before enter into their hearts to conceive.

### Those Who Do Not Walk after the Flesh

2. Now "whosoever abides in him, does not sin"; "does not walk after the flesh." The flesh, in the usual language of St. Paul, signifies corrupt nature. In this sense he uses the word, writing to the Galatians, "The works of the flesh are manifest" (Gal. 5:19); and a little before, "Walk in the Spirit, and you shall not fulfill the lust" (or desire) "of the flesh" (v. 16). To prove which, namely, that those who "walk by the Spirit," do not "fulfill the lusts of the flesh," he immediately adds, "For the flesh lusts against the Spirit, and the Spirit lusts against the flesh (for these are contrary to each other); that you may not do the things which you would." So the words are literally translated: ἵνα μὴ ἃ ἐὰν θέλητε ταῦτα ποιῆτε, not, "So that you cannot do the things that you would"; as if the flesh overcame the Spirit: a translation which has not only nothing to do with the original text of the Apostle, but likewise makes his whole argument worth nothing; indeed, asserts just the reverse of what he is proving.

3. They who are of Christ, who abide in him, "have crucified the flesh with its affections and lusts." They abstain from all those works of the flesh; from "adultery and fornication"; from "uncleanness and lasciviousness"; from "idolatry, witchcraft, hatred, contentions"; from "rivalry, wrath, strife, sedition, heresies, envy, murders, drunkenness, reveling"; from every design, and word, and work, to which the corruption of nature leads. Although they feel the root of bitterness in themselves, yet they are endued with power from on high to trample it continually under foot, so that it cannot "spring up to trouble them"; insomuch that every fresh assault which

they undergo only gives them fresh occasion of praise, of crying out, "Thanks be unto God, who gives us the victory through Jesus Christ our Lord."

## Those Who Walk after the Spirit

4. They now "walk after the Spirit," both in their hearts and lives. They are taught of him to love God and their neighbor, with a love that is as "a well of water, springing up into everlasting life." And by him they are led into every holy desire, into every divine and heavenly temper, till every thought that arises in their heart is holiness unto the Lord.

5. They who "walk after the Spirit," are also led by him into all holiness of conversation. Their "speech is always in grace, seasoned with salt"; with the love and fear of God. "No corrupt communication comes out of their mouth; but only that which is good," that which is "to the use of edifying," which is "meet to minister grace to the hearers." And in this likewise do they exercise themselves day and night, to do only the things which please God; in all their outward behavior to follow him "who left us an example that we might tread in his steps"; in all their interactions with their neighbor, to walk in justice, mercy, and truth; and "whatsoever they do," in every circumstances of life, to "do all to the glory of God."

6. These are they who indeed "walk after the Spirit." Being filled with faith and with the Holy Spirit, they possess in their hearts, and show forth in their lives—in the whole course of their words and actions—the genuine fruits of the Spirit of God, namely, "love, joy, peace, long-suffering, gentleness, goodness, fidelity, meekness, temperance," and whatsoever else is lovely or praiseworthy. "They adorn in all things the gospel of God our Savior"; and give full proof to all mankind, that they are indeed actuated by the same Spirit "who raised up Jesus from the dead."

## II. In What Way Is There No Condemnation for Those Who "Are in Christ"?

### *No Condemnation for Past Sins*

1. I proposed to show, in the second place, how "there is no condemnation to those who are" thus "in Christ Jesus," and thus "walk not after the flesh, but after the Spirit."

And, first, to believers in Christ, walking thus, "there is no condemnation" on account of their past sins. God does not condemn them for any of these; they are as though they had never been; they are cast "as a stone into the depth of the sea," and he remembers them no more. God, having "set forth his Son to be a propitiation" for them, "through faith in his blood," has declared unto them "his righteousness for the remission of the sins that are past." He lays therefore none of these to their charge; their memorial is perished with them.

2. And there is no condemnation in their own breast; no sense of guilt, or dread of the wrath of God. They "have the witness in themselves"; they are conscious of their interest in the blood of sprinkling. "They have not received again the spirit of bondage unto fear," unto doubt and racking uncertainty; but they "have received the Spirit of adoption," crying in their heart, "Abba, Father." Thus, being "justified by faith," they have the peace of God ruling in their hearts; flowing from a continual sense of his pardoning mercy, and "the answer of a good conscience toward God."

3. If it be said, "But sometimes a believer in Christ may lose his sight of the mercy of God; sometimes such darkness may fall upon him that he no longer sees him that is invisible, no longer feels that witness in himself of his part in the atoning blood; and then he is inwardly condemned, he has again "the sentence of death in himself." I answer, supposing it so to be, supposing him not to see the mercy

of God, then he is not a believer: for faith implies light, the
light of God shining upon the soul. So far, therefore, as any
one loses this light, he, for the time, loses his faith. And, no
doubt, a true believer in Christ may lose the light of faith;
and so far as this is lost, he may, for a time, fall again into
condemnation. But this is not the case of those who now
"are in Christ Jesus," who now believe in his name. For so
long as they believe, and walk after the Spirit, neither God
condemns them, nor their own heart.

## No Condemnation for Present Sins

4. They are not condemned, secondly, for any present
sins, for now transgressing the commandments of God. For
they do not transgress them: they do not "walk after the flesh,
but after the Spirit." This is the continual proof of their "love
of God, that they keep his commandments"; even as St. John
bears witness. "Whosoever is born of God does not commit
sin. For his seed remains in him, and he cannot sin, because
he is born of God"; he cannot, so long as that seed of God,
that loving, holy faith remains in him. So long as "he keeps
himself" in this, "that wicked one does not touch him."

Now it is evident, he is not condemned for the sins that
he does not commit at all. They, therefore, who are thus "led
by the Spirit, are not under the law" (Gal. 5:18): not under the
curse or condemnation of it; for it condemns none but those
who break it. Thus, that law of God, "You shall not steal,"
condemns none but those who do steal. Thus, "Remember
the Sabbath-day to keep it holy," condemns those only who
do not keep it holy. But against the fruits of the Spirit "there
is no law" (5:23); as the Apostle more largely declares in those
memorable words of his former Epistle to Timothy: "We
know that the law is good, if a man uses it lawfully; knowing
this"—if, while he uses the law of God, in order either to

convince or direct, he know and remember this—ὅτι δικαίῳ νόμος οὐ κεῖται (not, "that the law is not made for a righteous man," but "*that the law does not lie against a righteous man*": it has no force against him, no power to condemn him); "but against the lawless and disobedient, against the ungodly and sinners, against the unholy and profane; according to the glorious gospel of the blessed God" (1 Tim. 1:8–9, 11).

## No Condemnation for Remaining Inward Sin

5. They are not condemned, thirdly, for inward sin, even though it does now remain. That the corruption of nature does still remain, even in those who are the children of God by faith; that they have in them the seeds of pride and vanity, of anger, lust, and evil desire, indeed, sin of every kind; is too plain to be denied, being matter of daily experience. And on this account it is, that St. Paul, speaking to those whom he had just before witnessed to be "in Christ Jesus" (1 Cor. 1:2, 9), to have been "called of God into the fellowship" (or participation) "of his Son Jesus Christ"; yet declares, "Brethren, I could not speak unto you as unto spiritual, but as unto carnal, even as unto babes in Christ" (1 Cor. 3:1). "Babes in Christ"— so we see they were "in Christ"; they were believers in a low degree. And yet how much of sin remained in them! Of that "carnal mind, which is not subject to the law of God!"

6. And yet, for all this, they are not condemned. Although they feel the flesh, the evil nature, in them; although they are more sensible, day by day, that their "heart is deceitful and desperately wicked"; yet, so long as they do not yield to it; so long as they give no place to the devil; so long as they maintain a continual war with all sin, with pride, anger, desire, so that the flesh does not have dominion over them, but they still "walk after the Spirit"; "there is no condemnation to them which are in Christ Jesus." God is well pleased with

their sincere, though imperfect obedience; and they "have confidence toward God," knowing they are his, "by the Spirit which he has given" them (1 John 3:24).

## No Condemnation for Shortcomings in Holiness

7. Moreover, fourthly, although they are continually convinced of sin cleaving to all they do; although they are conscious of not fulfilling the perfect law, either in their thoughts, or words, or works; although they know they do not love the Lord their God with all their heart, and mind, and soul, and strength; although they feel more or less of pride, or self-will, stealing in, and mixing with their best duties; although even in their more immediate interactions with God, when they assemble themselves with the great congregation, and when they pour out their souls in secret to him who sees all the thoughts and intents of the heart, they are continually ashamed of their wandering thoughts, or of the deadness and dullness of their affections; yet there is no condemnation to them still, either from God or from their own heart. The consideration of these manifold defects only gives them a deeper sense, that they have always need of that blood of sprinkling which speaks for them in the ears of God, and that Advocate with the Father "who ever lives to make intercession for them." So far are these from driving them away from him in whom they have believed, that they rather drive them the closer to him whom they feel the want of every moment. And, at the same time, the deeper sense they have of this want, the more earnest desire do they feel, and the more diligent they are, as they "have received the Lord Jesus, so to walk in him."

## No Condemnation for Sins of Infirmity

8. They are not condemned, fifthly, for sins of infirmity, as they are usually called. Perhaps it would be advisable

rather to call them infirmities: that we may not seem to give any countenance to sin, or to extenuate it in any degree, by thus coupling it with infirmity. But (if we must retain so ambiguous and dangerous an expression), by sins of infirmity I would mean such involuntary failings as the saying a thing we believe true, though, in fact, it prove to be false; or, the hurting our neighbor without knowing or designing it, perhaps when we designed to do him good. Though these are deviations from the holy, and acceptable, and perfect will of God, yet they are not properly sins, nor do they bring any guilt on the conscience of "those who are in Christ Jesus." They do not separate between God and them, neither intercept the light of his countenance; as being in no way inconsistent with their general character of "walking not after the flesh, but after the Spirit."

## No Condemnation for Involuntary Sins

9. Lastly, "there is no condemnation" to them for anything whatsoever which it is not in their power to help; whether it be of an inward or outward nature, and whether it be doing something or leaving something undone. For instance, the Lord's Supper is to be administered; but you do not partake of it. Why do you not? You are confined by sickness; therefore, you cannot help omitting it; and for the same reason you are not condemned. There is no guilt, because there is no choice. As there "is a willing mind, it is accepted according to what a man has, not according to what he does not have."

10. A believer, indeed, may sometimes be grieved because he cannot do what his soul longs for. He may cry out, when he is detained from worshipping God in the great congregation, "Like as the deer pants after the water-brooks, so my soul pants after you, O God. My soul is athirst for

God, indeed, even for the living God. When shall I come to appear in the presence of God?" He may earnestly desire (only still saying in his heart, "Not as I will, but as you will") to "go again with the multitude, and bring them forth into the house of God." But still, if he cannot go, he feels no condemnation, no guilt, no sense of God's displeasure; but can cheerfully yield up those desires with, "O my soul, put your trust in God! For I will yet give him thanks, who is the help of my countenance and my God."

11. It is more difficult to determine concerning those which are usually styled sins of surprise: as when one who commonly in patience possesses his soul, on a sudden and violent temptation, speaks or acts in a manner not consistent with the royal law, "You shall love your neighbor as yourself." Perhaps it is not easy to fix a general rule concerning transgressions of this nature. We cannot say, either that men are, or that they are not, condemned for sins of surprise in general: but it seems whenever a believer is by surprise overtaken in a fault, there is more or less condemnation, as there is more or less concurrence of his will. In proportion as a sinful desire, or word, or action is more or less voluntary, so we may conceive God is more or less displeased, and there is more or less guilt upon the soul.

12. But if so, then there may be some sins of surprise that bring much guilt and condemnation. For, in some instances, our being surprised is owing to some wilfull and culpable neglect; or, to a sleepiness of soul that might have been prevented, or shaken off before the temptation came. A man may be previously warned either of God or man, that trials and dangers are at hand; and yet may say in his heart, "A little more slumber, a little more folding of the hands to rest." Now, if such a one afterward should fall, though unawares, into the snare which he might have avoided, that

he fell unawares, is no excuse; he might have foreseen and have shunned the danger. The falling, even by surprise, in such an instance as this, is, in effect, a willful sin; and, as such, must expose the sinner to condemnation, both from God and his own conscience.

13. On the other hand, there may be sudden assaults, either from the world, or the god of this world, and frequently from our own evil hearts, which we did not, and hardly could, foresee. And by these even a believer, while weak in faith, may possibly be borne down, suppose into a degree of anger, or thinking evil of another, with scarce any concurrence of his will. Now in such a case, the jealous God would undoubtedly show him that he had done foolishly. He would be convinced of having swerved from the perfect law, from the mind which was in Christ, and consequently, grieved with a godly sorrow, and lovingly ashamed before God.

Yet he need not come into condemnation. God does not lay folly to his charge, but has compassion upon him, "even as a father has compassion on his own children." And his heart does not condemn him: in the midst of that sorrow and shame he can still say, "I will trust and not be afraid; for the Lord Jehovah is my strength and my song; he also has become my salvation."

## III. Practical Inferences

### Those Who "Are in Christ" Shall Be Free and Unafraid

1. It remains only to draw some practical inferences from the preceding considerations. And, first, if there be "no condemnation to those who are in Christ Jesus," and "do not walk after the flesh, but after the Spirit," on account of their past sin; then why are you fearful, O you of little

faith? Though your sins were once more in number than the sand, what is that to you, now that you are in Christ Jesus? "Who shall lay anything to the charge of God's elect? It is God who justifies; who is he who condemns?" All the sins you have committed from your youth up, until the hour when you were "accepted in the Beloved," are driven away as chaff, are gone, are lost, swallowed up, remembered no more. You are now "born of the Spirit": Will you be troubled or afraid of what is done before you were born? Away with your fears! You are not called to fear, but to the "spirit of love and of a sound mind." Know your calling! Rejoice in God your Savior, and give thanks to God your Father through him!

2. Will you say, "But I have again committed sin, since I had redemption through his blood? And therefore it is, that "I abhor myself, and repent in dust and ashes." It is fitting you should abhor yourself; and it is God who has wrought you to this selfsame thing. But, do you now believe? Has he again enabled you to say, "I know that my Redeemer lives"; "and the life which I now live, I live by faith in the Son of God"? Then that faith again cancels all that is past, and there is no condemnation to you. At whatsoever time you truly believe in the name of the Son of God, all your sins, antecedent to that hour, vanish away as the morning dew.

Now then, "stand fast in the liberty wherewith Christ has made you free." He has once more made you free from the power of sin, as well as from the guilt and punishment of it. O "do not be entangled again with the yoke of bondage!"—neither the vile, devilish bondage of sin, of evil desires, evil tempers, or words, or works, the most grievous yoke on this side hell; nor the bondage of slavish, tormenting fear, of guilt and self-condemnation.

## Those Who Commit Sin Are Not "in Christ"

3. But secondly, do all those who abide "in Christ Jesus, walk not after the flesh, but after the Spirit"? Then we cannot but infer, that whosoever now commits sin, has no part or lot in this matter. He is even now condemned by his own heart. But, "if our heart condemns us," if our own conscience bears witness that we are guilty, undoubtedly God does; for "he is greater than our heart, and knows all things"; so that we cannot deceive him, if we can ourselves.

And think not to say, "I was justified once; my sins were once forgiven me": I do not know that; neither will I dispute whether they were or not. Perhaps, at this distance of time, it is next to impossible to know, with any tolerable degree of certainty, whether that was a true, genuine work of God, or whether you did only deceive your own soul. But this I know, with the utmost degree of certainty: "he that commits sin is of the devil." Therefore, you are of your father, the devil. It cannot be denied: for you do the works of your father.

O do not flatter yourself with vain hopes! Say not to your soul, "Peace, peace!" For there is no peace. Cry aloud! Cry unto God out of the deep; if by chance he may hear your voice. Come unto him as at first, as wretched and poor, as sinful, miserable, blind and naked! And beware you suffer your soul to take no rest, till his pardoning love be again revealed; till he "heal your backslidings," and fill you again with the "faith that works by love."

## Those Who Know Their Sin Shall Find Hope in God

4. Thirdly, is there no condemnation to those who "walk after the Spirit," by reason of inward sin still remaining, so long as they do not give way to it; nor by reason of sin cleaving to all they do? Then do not fret because of ungodliness,

though it still remain in your heart. Repine not, because you still come short of the glorious image of God; nor yet because pride, self-will, or unbelief, cleave to all your words and works. And be not afraid to know all this evil of your heart, to know yourself as also you are known. Indeed, desire of God, that you may not think of yourself more highly than you ought to think. Let your continual prayer be,

*Show me, as my soul can bear,*
*The depth of inbred sin;*
*All the unbelief declare,*
*The pride that lurks within.*

But when he hears your prayer, and unveils your heart; when he shows you thoroughly of what spirit you are; then beware that your faith does not fail you, that you suffer not your shield to be torn from you. Be abased. Be humbled in the dust. See yourself as nothing, less than nothing, and vanity. But still, "Let not your heart be troubled, neither let it be afraid." Still hold fast, "I, even I, have an Advocate with the Father, Jesus Christ the righteous." "And as the heavens are higher than the earth, so is his love—higher than even my sins."

Therefore, God is merciful to you a sinner! Such a sinner as you are! God is love; and Christ has died! Therefore, the Father himself loves you! You are his child! Therefore he will withhold from you no manner of thing that is good. Is it good, that the whole body of sin, which is now crucified in you, should be destroyed? It shall be done! You shall be "cleansed from all filthiness, both of flesh and spirit." Is it good, that nothing should remain in your heart but the pure love of God alone? Be of good cheer! "You shall love the Lord your God, with all your heart, and mind, and soul, and strength." "Faithful is he who has promised, who also will do it." It is your part, patiently to continue in the work of faith, and in the labor of love; and in cheerful peace, in humble confidence, with calm and resigned and yet earnest expectation, to wait till the zeal of the Lord of hosts shall perform this.

## Do Not Let Involuntary Sins Become an Opportunity for Satan

5. Fourthly, if those who "are in Christ," and "walk after the Spirit," are not condemned for sins of infirmity; as neither for involuntary failings, nor for anything whatsoever which they are not able to help; then beware, O you that have faith in his blood, that Satan herein gains no advantage over you. You are still foolish and weak, blind and ignorant; more weak than any words can express; more foolish than it can yet enter into your heart to conceive; knowing nothing yet as you ought to know. Yet let not all your weakness and folly, or any fruit of these, which you are not yet able to avoid, shake your faith, your filial trust in God, or disturb your peace or joy in the Lord.

The rule which some give, as to willful sins, and which, in that case, may perhaps be dangerous, is undoubtedly wise and safe if it be applied only to the case of weakness and infirmities. Are you fallen, O man of God? Yet, do not lie there, fretting and bemoaning your weakness; but meekly say, "Lord, I shall fall every moment, unless you uphold me with your hand." And then arise! Leap and walk! Go on your way! "Run with patience the race that is set before you."

## Those Overtaken by Their Faults Should Grieve unto the Lord

6. Lastly, since a believer need not come into condemnation, even though he be surprised into what his soul abhors

(suppose his being surprised is not owing to any carelessness or willful neglect of his own); if you who believe are thus overtaken in a fault, then grieve unto the Lord; it shall be a precious balm. Pour out your heart before him, and show him of your trouble, and pray with all your might to him who is "touched with the feeling of your infirmities," that he would establish, and strengthen, and settle your soul, and suffer you to fall no more.

But still he does not condemn you. Why should you fear? You have no need of any "fear that has torment." You shall love him who loves you, and it suffices: more love will bring more strength. And, as soon as you love him with all your heart, you shall be perfect and entire, lacking nothing. "Wait in peace for that hour, when the God of peace shall sanctify you wholly, so that your whole spirit and soul and body may be preserved blameless unto the coming of our Lord Jesus Christ!"

# FOUR

# The Way to the Kingdom

## 1746

*"The kingdom of God is at hand: repent, and believe the gospel."*

—Mark 1:15

## Introduction

These words naturally lead us to consider, first, the nature of true religion, here termed by our Lord, "the kingdom of God," which, he says, "is at hand"; and, secondly, the way to it, which he points out in those words, "Repent, and believe the gospel."

## I. The Nature of True Religion

1. We are, first, to consider the nature of true religion, here termed by our Lord, "the kingdom of God." The great Apostle uses the same expression in his Epistle to the

Romans, where he likewise explains his Lord's words, saying, "The kingdom of God is not meat and drink; but righteousness, and peace, and joy in the Holy Spirit" (Rom. 14:17).

## The Kingdom of God Is Not in Any Outward Thing

2. "The kingdom of God," or true religion, "is not meat and drink." It is well known that not only the unconverted Jews, but also great numbers of those who had received the faith of Christ, were, notwithstanding "zealous of the law" (Acts 21:20), even the ceremonial law of Moses. Whatever, therefore, they found written in it, either concerning meat and drink offerings, or the distinction between clean and unclean meats, they not only observed themselves, but vehemently pressed the same even on those "among the Gentiles" (or heathens) "who were turned to God"; indeed, to such a degree, that some of them taught, wherever they came among them, "Unless you are circumcised, and keep the law" (the whole ritual law), "you cannot be saved" (Acts 15:1, 24).

3. In opposition to these, the Apostle declares, both here and in many other places, that true religion does not consist in *meat* and *drink*, or in any ritual observances; nor, indeed in any outward thing whatsoever; in anything exterior to the heart; the whole substance thereof lying in "righteousness, peace, and joy in the Holy Ghost."

4. Not in any *outward thing*; such as *forms*, or *ceremonies*, even of the most excellent kind. Supposing these to be ever so decent and significant, ever so expressive of inward things; supposing them ever so helpful, not only to the common men, whose thought reaches little farther than their sight; but even to men of understanding, men of strong capacities, as doubtless they may sometimes be: indeed, supposing them, as in the case of the Jews, to be appointed by God himself; yet even during the period of time in which that

appointment remains in force, true religion does not principally consist therein; indeed, strictly speaking, not at all.

How much more must this hold concerning such rites and forms as are only of human appointment! The religion of Christ rises infinitely higher, and lies immensely deeper, than all these. These are good in their place, just so far as they are in fact subservient to true religion. And it would be superstition to object against them, while they are applied only as occasional helps to human weakness. But let no man carry them farther. Let no man dream that they have any intrinsic worth; or that religion cannot subsist without them. This would be to make them an abomination to the Lord.

5. The nature of religion is so far from consisting in these, in forms of worship, or rites and ceremonies, that it does not properly consist in any outward actions of any kind whatsoever. It is true, a man cannot have any religion who is guilty of vicious, immoral actions; or who does to others what he would not want them to do to him, if he were in the same circumstance. And it is also true, that he can have no real religion who "knows to do good, and does not do it." Yet a man may both abstain from outward evil, and do good, and still have no religion. Indeed, two persons may do the same outward work; suppose, feeding the hungry, or clothing the naked; and, in the meantime, one of these may be truly religious, and the other have no religion at all: for the one may act from the love of God, and the other from the love of praise. So it is clearly shown, that although true religion naturally leads to every good word and work, yet the real nature of it lies deeper still, even in "the hidden man of the heart."

6. I say of *the heart*, for neither does religion consist in orthodoxy, or right opinions; which, although they are not properly outward things, are not in the heart, but the

understanding. A man may be orthodox in every point; he may not only espouse right opinions, but zealously defend them against all opponents; he may think justly concerning the incarnation of our Lord, concerning the ever-blessed Trinity, and every other doctrine contained in the oracles of God; he may assent to all the three creeds—that called the Apostles', the Nicene, and the Athanasian; and yet it is possible he may have no religion at all, no more than a Jew, Turk, or pagan. He may be almost as orthodox—as the devil (though, indeed, not altogether; for every man errs in something; whereas we can't well conceive him to hold any erroneous opinion), and may, all the while be as great a stranger as he to the religion of the heart.

## The Kingdom of God Is Righteousness

7. This alone is religion, truly so called; this alone is in the sight of God of great price. The Apostle sums it all up in three particulars, "righteousness, and peace, and joy in the Holy Spirit." First, *righteousness*. We cannot be at a loss concerning this, if we remember the words of our Lord, describing the two grand branches of it, on which "hang all the law and the prophets": "You shall love the Lord your God with all your heart, and with all your mind, and with all your soul, and with all your strength: this is the first and great commandment" (Mark 12:30), the first and great branch of Christian righteousness.

You shall delight yourself in the Lord your God; you shall seek and find all happiness in him. He shall be "your shield, and your exceeding great reward," in time and in eternity. All your bones shall say, "Whom have I in heaven but you? And there is none upon earth that I desire beside you!" You shall hear and fulfill his word who says, "My son, give me your heart." And, having given him your heart, your inmost soul, to reign there without a rival, you may well cry out, in the fullness of your heart, "I will love you, O Lord, my strength. The Lord is my strong rock, and my defense; my Savior, my God, and my might, in whom I will trust; my shield, the horn also of my salvation, and my refuge."

8. And the second commandment is like unto this; the second great branch of Christian righteousness is closely and inseparably connected with it; even, "You shall love your neighbour as yourself." *You shall love*—you shall embrace with the most tender good-will, the most earnest and cordial affection, the most inflamed desires of preventing or removing all evil, and of procuring for him every possible good.

*Your neighbor*—that is, not only your friend, your kinsman, or your acquaintance; not only the virtuous, the friendly, he who loves you, who prevents or returns your kindness; but every child of man, every human creature, every soul which God has made; not excluding him whom you never have seen in the flesh, whom you do not know, either by face or name; not excluding him who you know to be evil and unthankful, he who still despitefully uses and persecutes you—him you shall love *as yourself;* with the same invariable thirst after his happiness in every kind; the same unwearied care to screen him from whatever might grieve or hurt either his soul or body.

9. Now is this not love "the fulfilling of the law," the sum of all Christian righteousness?—of all inward righteousness; for it necessarily implies "tender mercies (NKJV), humbleness of mind" (seeing "love is not puffed up"), "gentleness, meekness, long-suffering" (for love "is not provoked," but "believes, hopes, endures all things"); and of all outward righteousness; for "love does not work evil to his neighbor," either by word or deed. It cannot willingly hurt or grieve anyone. And it is zealous of good works. Every lover of

mankind, as he has opportunity, "does good unto all men," being (without partiality and without hypocrisy) "full of mercy and good fruits."

## *The Kingdom of God Is Peace and Joy*

10. But true religion, or a heart right toward God and man, implies happiness as well as holiness. For it is not only "righteousness," but also "peace and joy in the Holy Spirit." What peace? "The peace of God," which only God can give, and the world cannot take away; the peace which "passes all understanding," all barely rational conception; being a supernatural sensation, a divine taste, of "the powers of the world to come"; such as the natural man does not know, however wise in the things of this world; nor, indeed, can he know it, in his present state, "because it is spiritually discerned."

It is a peace that banishes all doubt, all painful uncertainty; the Spirit of God bearing witness with the spirit of a Christian, that he is "a child of God." And it banishes fear, all such fear as has torment; the fear of the wrath of God; the fear of hell; the fear of the devil; and, in particular, the fear of death: he who has the peace of God, desiring, if it were the will of God, "to depart, and to be with Christ."

11. With this peace of God, wherever it is fixed in the soul, there is also "joy in the Holy Spirit"—joy wrought in the heart by the Holy Spirit, by the ever-blessed Spirit of God. It is he who works in us that calm, humble rejoicing in God, through Christ Jesus, "by whom we have now received the atonement," καταλλαγὴν, *the reconciliation with God*; and who enables us boldly to confirm the truth of the royal Psalmist's declaration, "Blessed" (or rather, *happy*) "is the man whose unrighteousness is forgiven, and whose sin is covered." He it is who inspires the Christian soul with that even, solid joy, which arises from the testimony of the Spirit

that he is a child of God; and that gives him to "rejoice with joy unspeakable, in hope of the glory of God"; hope both of the glorious image of God, which is in part and shall be fully "revealed in him"; and of that crown of glory which does not fade away, reserved in heaven for him.

### The Kingdom of God Is Holiness and Happiness Joined in One

12. This holiness and happiness, joined in one, are sometimes styled, in the inspired writings, "the kingdom of God" (as by our Lord in the text), and sometimes, "the kingdom of heaven." It is termed "the kingdom of God," because it is the immediate fruit of God's reigning in the soul. As soon as ever he takes unto himself his mighty power, and sets up his throne in our hearts, they are instantly filled with this "righteousness, and peace, and joy in the Holy Spirit." It is called "the kingdom of heaven" because it is (in a degree) heaven opened in the soul. For whosoever they are that experience this, they can declare before angels and men,

> *Everlasting life is won,*
> *Glory is on earth begun,*

according to the constant tenor of Scripture, which everywhere bears record, God "has given unto us eternal life, and this life is in his Son. He that has the Son" (reigning in his heart) "has life," even life everlasting (1 John 5:11–12). For "this is life eternal, to know you, the only true God, and Jesus Christ, whom you have sent" (John 17:3). And they, to whom this is given, may confidently address God, though they were in the midst of a fiery furnace,

> *Thee, Lord, safe shielded by thy power,*
> *Thee, Son of God, JEHOVAH, we adore;*

*In form of man descending to appear:*
*To thee be ceaseless hallelujahs given,*
*Praise, as in heaven thy throne, we offer here;*
*For where thy presence is display'd, is heaven.*

## The Kingdom of God Is at Hand

13. And this "kingdom of God," or of heaven, "is at hand." As these words were originally spoken, they implied that "the time" was then fulfilled, God being "made manifest in the flesh," when he would set up his kingdom among men, and reign in the hearts of his people. And is not the time now fulfilled? For, "Lo!" (he says), "I am with you always"—you who preach remission of sins in my name—"even unto the end of the world" (Matt. 28:20). Wherever, therefore, the gospel of Christ is preached, this his "kingdom is near at hand." It is not far from every one of you. You may this hour enter into it, if you hearken to his voice: "Repent, and believe the gospel."

# II. The Way to the Kingdom

## Repent: Know Your Utter Corruption

1. This is the way: walk in it. And, first, "repent"; that is, know yourselves. This is the first repentance, previous to faith; even conviction, or self-knowledge. Awake, then, you who sleep. Know yourself to be a sinner, and what manner of sinner you are. Know that corruption of your inmost nature, by which you are very far gone from original righteousness, by which "the flesh lusts" always "contrary to the Spirit," through that "carnal mind" which "is enmity against God," which "is not subject to the law of God, neither indeed can be."

Know that you are corrupted in every power, in every faculty of your soul; that you are totally corrupted in every one of these, all the foundations being out of course. The eyes of your understanding are darkened, so that they cannot discern God, or the things of God. The clouds of ignorance and error rest upon you, and cover you with the shadow of death. You know nothing yet as you ought to know—neither God, nor the world, nor yourself.

Your will is no longer the will of God, but is utterly perverse and distorted, averse from all good, from all which God loves, and prone to all evil, to every abomination which God hates. Your affections are alienated from God, and scattered abroad over all the earth. All your passions, both your desires and aversions, your joys and sorrows, your hopes and fears, are out of frame, are either undue in their degree, or placed on undue objects. So that there is no soundness in your soul; but "from the crown of the head, to the sole of the foot" (to use the strong expression of the Prophet), there are only "wounds, and bruises, and putrefying sores."

2. Such is the inbred corruption of your heart, of your very inmost nature. And what manner of branches can you expect to grow from such an evil root? From this springs unbelief; ever departing from the living God, saying, "Who is the Lord, that I should serve him? Tush! You, God, do not care for it." From this, independence; aiming to be like the Most High. From this, pride, in all its forms; teaching you to say, "I am rich, and increased in goods, and have need of nothing." From this evil fountain flow forth the bitter streams of vanity, thirst of praise, ambition, covetousness, the lust of the flesh, the lust of the eye, and the pride of life. From this arise anger, hatred, malice, revenge, envy, jealousy, evil surmising; from this, all the foolish and hurtful lusts that now "pierce you through with many sorrows," and if not timely prevented, will at length drown your soul in everlasting perdition.

3. And what fruits can grow on such branches as these? Only such as are bitter and evil continually. From pride come

contention, vain boasting, seeking and receiving praise of men, and so robbing God of that glory which he cannot give unto another. From the lust of the flesh, come gluttony or drunkenness, luxury or sensuality, fornication, uncleanness; variously defiling that body which was designed for a temple of the Holy Spirit; of unbelief, every evil word and work.

But the time would fail, should you reckon up all; all the idle words you have spoken, provoking the Most High, grieving the Holy One of Israel; all the evil works you have done, either wholly evil in themselves, or, at least, not done to the glory of God. For your actual sins are more than you are able to express, more than the hairs of your head. Who can number the sands of the sea, or the drops of rain, or your iniquities?

## *Repent: Know Your Guilt and Helplessness*

4. And do you not know that "the wages of sin is death"— death, not only temporal, but eternal? "The soul that sins, it shall die"; "for the mouth of the Lord has spoken it." It shall die the second death. This is the sentence: to "be punished" with never-ending death, "with everlasting destruction from the presence of the Lord, and from the glory of his power." Do you not know that every sinner, ἔνοχος ἔσται εἰς τὴν γέενναν τοῦ πυρός, not properly, *is in danger of hell-fire*, is far too weak; but rather, *is under the sentence of hell-fire*; doomed already, just dragging to execution.

You are guilty of everlasting death. It is the just reward of your inward and outward wickedness. It is just that the sentence should now take place. Do you see, do you feel this? Are you thoroughly convinced that you deserve God's wrath and everlasting damnation? Would God do you no wrong, if he now commanded the earth to open and swallow you up? If you were now to go down quick into the pit, into the fire that never shall be quenched? If God has given you truly to repent, you have a deep sense that these things are so; and that it is of his mere mercy you are not consumed, swept away from the face of the earth.

5. And what will you do to appease the wrath of God, to atone for all your sins, and to escape the punishment you have so justly deserved? Alas, you can do nothing; nothing that will in any way make amends to God for one evil work, or word, or thought. If you could now do all things well, if from this very hour, till your soul should return to God you could perform perfect, uninterrupted obedience, even this would not atone for what is past. The not increasing your debt would not discharge it. It would still remain as great as ever. Indeed, the present and future obedience of all the men upon earth, and all the angels in heaven, would never make satisfaction to the justice of God for one single sin. How vain, then, was the thought of atoning for your own sins, by anything you could do! It cost far more to redeem one soul, than all mankind is able to pay. So that were there no other help for a guilty sinner, without doubt he must have perished everlastingly.

6. But suppose perfect obedience, for the time to come, could atone for the sins that are past, this would profit you nothing; for you are not able to perform it; no, not in any one point. Begin now: make the trial. Shake off that outward sin that so easily besets you. You cannot. How then will you change your life from all evil to all good? Indeed, it is impossible to be done, unless first your heart is changed. For, so long as the tree remains evil, it cannot bring forth good fruit. But are you able to change your own heart, from all sin to all holiness? To revive a soul that is dead in sin—dead to God and alive only to the world?

No more than you are able to revive a dead body, to raise to life him who lies in the grave. Indeed, you are not able to revive your soul in any degree, no more than to give any degree of life to the dead body. You can do nothing, more or less, in this matter; you are utterly without strength. To be deeply sensible of this, how helpless you are, as well as how guilty and how sinful—this is that "repentance not to be repented of," which is the forerunner of the kingdom of God.

7. If to this lively conviction of your inward and outward sins, of your utter guiltiness and helplessness, there be added suitable affections—sorrow of heart, for having despised your own mercies; remorse and self-condemnation, having your mouth stopped; shame to lift up your eyes to heaven; fear of the wrath of God abiding on you, of his curse hanging over your head, and of the fiery indignation ready to devour those who forget God, and obey not our Lord Jesus Christ; earnest desire to escape from that indignation, to cease from evil, and learn to do well—then I say unto you, in the name of the Lord, "You are not far from the kingdom of God." One step more and you shall enter in. You do "repent." Now, "believe the gospel."

## Believe the Good News for Sinners

8. *The gospel* (that is, good tidings, good news for guilty, helpless sinners), in the largest sense of the word, means the whole revelation made to men by Jesus Christ; and sometimes the whole account of what our Lord did and suffered while he tabernacled among men. The substance of all is, "Jesus Christ came into the world to save sinners"; or, "God so loved the world that he gave his only-begotten Son, to the end we might not perish, but have everlasting life"; or, "He was bruised for our transgressions, he was wounded for our iniquities; the chastisement of our peace was upon him; and with his wounds we are healed."

9. *Believe* this, and the kingdom of God is yours. By faith you attain the promise. "He pardons and absolves all who truly repent, and genuinely believe his holy gospel."

As soon as ever God has spoken to your heart, "Be of good cheer, your sins are forgiven you," his kingdom comes: you have "righteousness, and peace, and joy in the Holy Spirit."

10. Only beware you do not deceive your own soul with regard to the nature of this faith. It is not, as some have fondly conceived, a bare assent to the truth of the Bible, of the articles of our creed, or of all that is contained in the Old and New Testament. The devils believe this, as well as I or you! And yet they are devils still. But it is, over and above this, a sure trust in the mercy of God, through Christ Jesus. It is a confidence in a pardoning God. It is a divine evidence or conviction that "God was in Christ, reconciling the world to himself, not imputing to them their" former "trespasses"; and, in particular, that the Son of God has loved *me,* and given himself for *me;* and that I, even I, am now reconciled to God by the blood of the cross.

11. Do you thus believe? Then the peace of God is in your heart, and sorrow and sighing flee away. You are no longer in doubt of the love of God; it is clear as the noon-day sun. You cry out, "My song shall be always of the loving-kindness of the Lord: With my mouth will I ever be telling of your truth, from one generation to another." You are no longer afraid of hell, or death, or him that had once the power of death, the devil; no, nor painfully afraid of God himself; only you have a tender, filial fear of offending him.

Do you believe? Then your "soul does magnify the Lord," and your "spirit rejoices in God your Savior." You rejoice in that you have "redemption through his blood, even the forgiveness of sins." You rejoice in that "Spirit of adoption," which cries in your heart, "Abba, Father!" You rejoice in a "hope full of immortality"; in reaching forth unto the "mark of the prize of your high calling"; in an earnest expectation of all the good things which God has prepared for them that love him.

12. Do you now believe? Then "the love of God is" now "shed abroad in your heart." You love him, because he first loved us. And because you love God, you love your brother also. And being filled with "love, peace, joy," you are also filled with "long-suffering, gentleness, fidelity, goodness, meekness, temperance," and all the other fruits of the same Spirit; in a word, with whatever dispositions are holy, are heavenly or divine. For while you "behold with open," uncovered "face" (the veil now being taken away) "the glory of the Lord," his glorious love, and the glorious image in which you were created, you are "changed into the same image, from glory to glory, by the Spirit of the Lord."

13. This repentance, this faith, this peace, joy, love, this change from glory to glory, is what the wisdom of the world has voted to be madness, mere enthusiasm, utter distraction. But you, O man of God, regard them not; be moved by none of these things. You know in whom you have believed. See that no man takes your crown. Hold fast to what you have already attained, and follow, till you attain all the great and precious promises.

And you who have not yet known him, let not vain men make you ashamed of the gospel of Christ. Be in nothing terrified by those who speak evil of the things which they do not know. God will soon turn your heaviness into joy. O let not your hands hang down! Yet a little longer, and he will take away your fears, and give you the spirit of a sound mind. He is near "who justifies: Who is he that condemns? It is Christ that died, indeed rather, that rose again, who is even now at the right hand of God, making intercession" for you. "Now cast yourself on the Lamb of God, with all your sins, how ever many they may be; and "an entrance shall" now "be ministered unto you, into the kingdom of our Lord and Savior Jesus Christ!"

# FIVE

# Marks of the New Birth

## 1748

*"So is every one that is born of the Spirit."*

—John 3:8

## Introduction

1. How is every one that is "born of the Spirit"—that is, born again—born of God? What is meant by being born again, being born of God, or being born of the Spirit? What is implied in being a son or a child of God, or having the Spirit of adoption? That these privileges, by the free mercy of God, are ordinarily annexed to baptism (which is termed by our Lord in a preceding verse, the being "born of water and of the Spirit") we know; but we wish to know what these privileges are: What is the new birth?

2. Perhaps it is not needful to give a definition of this, seeing the Scripture gives none. But as the question is of the

deepest concern to every child of man; since, "unless a man be born again," born of the Spirit, "he cannot see the kingdom of God"; I propose to lay down the marks of it in the plainest manner, just as I find them laid down in Scripture.

## I. The New Birth Is Marked by Faith

1. The first of these, and the foundation of all the rest, is faith. So St. Paul: "You are all the children of God by faith in Christ Jesus" (Gal. 3:26). So St. John: "To them he gave power" (ἐξουσίαν, *right* or *privilege,* it might rather be translated) "to become the sons of God, even to them who believe on his name; which were born," when they believed, "not of blood, nor of the will of the flesh"; not by natural generation, "nor of the will of man," like those children adopted by men, in whom no inward change is thereby wrought; "but of God" (John 1:12–13). And again in his General Epistle: "Whosoever believes that Jesus is the Christ is born of God" (1 John 5:1).

### Faith Is Not Mere Assent, but Disposition and Confidence

2. But it is not a barely notional or speculative faith that is here spoken of by the Apostles. It is not a bare assent to this proposition, Jesus is the Christ; nor indeed to all the propositions contained in our creed, or in the Old and New Testament. It is not merely an assent to any or all these credible things, as credible. To say this, were to say (which who could hear?) that the devils were born of God, for they have this faith. They, trembling, believe both that Jesus is the Christ, and that all Scripture, having been given by inspiration of God, is true as God is true.

It is not only an assent to divine truth, upon the testimony of God, or upon the evidence of miracles; for *they* also heard the words of his mouth, and knew him to be a faithful and true witness. They could not but receive the testimony he gave, both of himself, and of the Father who sent him. They saw likewise the mighty works that he did, and thus believed that he "came forth from God." Yet, notwithstanding this faith, they are still "reserved in chains of darkness unto the judgment of the great day."

3. For all this is no more than a dead faith. The true, living, Christian faith (whosoever has it, is born of God), is not only an assent, an act of the understanding; but a disposition, which God has wrought in his heart: "a sure trust and confidence in God, that, through the merits of Christ, his sins are forgiven, and he is reconciled to the favor of God."

This implies that a man first renounces himself; that, in order to be "found in Christ," to be accepted through him, he totally rejects all "confidence in the flesh"; that, "having nothing to pay," having no trust in his own works or righteousness of any kind, he comes to God as a lost, miserable, self-destroyed, self-condemned, undone, helpless sinner; as one whose mouth is utterly stopped, and who is altogether "guilty before God."

Such a sense of sin (commonly called despair, by those who speak evil of the things they know not), together with a full conviction, such as no words can express, that of Christ only comes our salvation, and an earnest desire of that salvation, must precede a living faith, a trust in him, who "for us paid our ransom by his death, and fulfilled the law of his life." This faith then, by which we are born of God, is "not only a belief of all the articles of our faith, but also a true confidence of the mercy of God, through our Lord Jesus Christ."

## *Faith Bears the Fruit of Power over Sin*

4. An immediate and constant fruit of this faith by which we are born of God, a fruit which can in no way be separated from it, no, not for an hour, is power over sin—power over outward sin of every kind; over every evil word and work; for wherever the blood of Christ is thus applied, it "purges the conscience from dead works"—and over inward sin, for it purifies the heart from every unholy desire and temper.

This fruit of faith St. Paul has largely described, in the sixth chapter of his Epistle to the Romans. "How shall we," he says, "who" by faith "are dead to sin, live any longer in it?" "Our old man is crucified with Christ, that the body of sin might be destroyed, that henceforth we should not serve sin." "Likewise, reckon yourselves to be dead unto sin, but alive unto God, through Jesus Christ our Lord. Let not sin therefore reign" even "in your mortal body," "but yield yourselves unto God, as those that are alive from the dead." "For sin shall not have dominion over you. God be thanked, that you were the servants of sin . . . but being made free"—the plain meaning is, God be thanked that though you were, in time past, the servants of sin, yet now—"being free from sin, you have become the servants of righteousness."

5. The same invaluable privilege of the sons of God is as strongly asserted by St. John; particularly with regard to the former branch of it, namely, power over outward sin. After he had been crying out, as one astonished at the depth of the riches of the goodness of God—"Behold, what manner of love the Father has bestowed upon us, that we should be called the sons of God! Beloved, now we are the sons of God, and it does not yet appear what we shall be; but we know, that when he shall appear, we shall be like him; for we shall see him as he is" (1 John 3:1–2)—he soon adds, "Whoever is

born of God does not commit sin; for his seed remains in him: and he cannot sin, because he is born of God" (v. 9).

But some men will say, "True: Whoever is born of God does not commit sin *habitually.*" *Habitually!* Where is that? I do not read it. It is not written in the Book. God plainly says, "He does not commit sin"; and you add, *habitually!* Who are you who *mend* the oracles of God—who "add to the words of this book?" Beware; I beseech you, lest God "add to you all the plagues that are written in it!" Especially when the comment you add is such as quite swallows up the text; so that by this μεθοδεία πλάνης, *artful method of deceiving*, the precious promise is utterly lost; by this κυβεία ἀνθρώπων, *tricking and shuffling of men*, the word of God is made of none effect. O beware, you who thus take from the words of this book, that, taking away the whole meaning and spirit from them, leave only what may indeed be termed a dead letter, lest God take away your part out of the book of life!

6. We allow the Apostle to interpret his own words, by the whole tenor of his discourse. In the fifth verse of this chapter, he had said, "You know that he," Christ, "was manifested to take away our sins; and in him is no sin." What is the inference he draws from this? "Whoever abides in him does not sin. Whoever sins has not seen him, neither known him" (1 John 3:6). To his enforcement of this important doctrine, he premises a highly necessary caution: "Little children, let no man deceive you" (v. 7); for many will endeavor to do so—to persuade you that you may be unrighteous, that you may commit sin, and yet be children of God!

"He that does righteousness is righteous, even as he is righteous. He that commits sin is of the devil; for the devil sins from the beginning." Then follows, "Whoever is born of God does not commit sin; for his seed remains in him:

and he cannot sin, because he is born of God. In this," adds the Apostle, "the children of God are manifest, and the children of the devil." By this plain mark (the committing or not committing sin) are they distinguished from each other. To the same effect are those words in his fifth chapter, "We know that whosoever is born of God sins not; but he that is born of God keeps himself, and that wicked one does not touch him" (1 John 5:18).

## *Faith Bears the Fruit of Unshakable Peace*

7. Another fruit of this living faith is peace. For, "being justified by faith," having all our sins blotted out, "we have peace with God, through our Lord Jesus Christ" (Rom. 5:1). This indeed our Lord himself, the night before his death, solemnly bequeathed to all his followers: "Peace," he says, "I leave with you" (you who "believe in God," and "believe also in me"); "My peace I give to you; not as the world gives do I give to you. Let not your heart be troubled, neither let it be afraid" (John 14:27 NKJV). And again, "These things have I spoken to you, that in me you might have peace" (John 16:33).

This is that "peace of God which passes all understanding," that serenity of soul which it has not entered into the heart of a natural man to conceive, and which it is not possible for even the spiritual man to utter. And it is a peace that all the powers of earth and hell are unable to take from him. Waves and storms beat upon it, but they do not shake it; for it is founded upon a rock. It keeps the hearts and minds of the children of God, at all times and in all places. Whether they are in ease or in pain, in sickness or health, in abundance or want, they are happy in God. In every state they have learned to be content, indeed, to give thanks unto God through Christ Jesus; being well assured that "whatever is, is best," because it is his will concerning them: so that in all the vicissitudes of life their "heart stands fast, believing in the Lord."

## II. The New Birth Is Marked by Hope

1. A second scriptural mark of those who are born of God is hope. Thus St. Peter, speaking to all the children of God who were then scattered abroad, says, "Blessed be the God and Father of our Lord Jesus Christ, who, according to his abundant mercy, has given us new birth into a lively hope" (1 Peter 1:3). Ελπίδα ζῶσαν, *a lively or living hope*, says the Apostle; because there is also a *dead* hope, as well as a dead faith; a hope which is not from God, but from the enemy of God and man, as evidently appears by its fruits; for, as it is the offspring of pride, so it is the parent of every evil word and work; whereas, every man that has in him this living hope, is "holy as he who calls him is holy." Every man who can truly say to his brothers in Christ, "Beloved, now are we the sons of God, and we shall see him as he is," "purifies himself, even as he is pure."

2. This hope implies, first, the testimony of our own spirit or conscience, that we walk "in simplicity and godly sincerity"; secondly, the testimony of the Spirit of God, "bearing witness with," or to, "our spirit, that we are the children of God," "and if children, then heirs, heirs of God, and joint-heirs with Christ."

### Hope Bears Witness that We Are Children of God

3. Let us well observe what is here taught us by God himself, touching this glorious privilege of his children. Who is it that is here said to bear witness? Not our spirit only, but another; even the Spirit of God: It is he who "bears witness with our spirit." What is it he bears witness of? "That we are

the children of God," "and if children, then heirs; heirs of God, and joint-heirs with Christ" (Rom. 8:16–17); "if indeed we suffer with him," if we deny ourselves, if we take up our cross daily, if we cheerfully endure persecution or reproach for his sake, "that we may also be glorified together."

And in whom does the Spirit of God bear this witness? In all who are the children of God. By this very argument does the Apostle prove, in the preceding verses, that they are so: "As many," he says, "as are led by the Spirit of God, they are the sons of God." "For you have not received the spirit of bondage again to fear; but you have received the Spirit of adoption, by which we cry, Abba, Father!" It follows, "The Spirit itself bears witness with our spirit, that we are the children of God" (Rom. 8:14–16).

4. The variation of the phrase in the fifteenth verse is worthy our observation: "You have received the Spirit of adoption, by which we cry, Abba, Father!" *You*, as many as are the sons of God, have, by virtue of your sonship, received that selfsame Spirit of adoption, whereby *we* cry, Abba, Father—*we*, the apostles, prophets, teachers (for so the word may not improperly be understood)—*we*, through whom you have believed, the "ministers of Christ, and stewards of the mysteries of God." As *we* and *you* have one Lord, so we have one Spirit: as we have one faith, so we have one hope also. We and you are sealed with one "Spirit of promise," the earnest of *your* and of *our* inheritance: the same Spirit bearing witness with your and with our spirit, "that we are the children of God" (Rom. 8:14–16).

## *Hope Bears the Fruit of Rejoicing, Even in Affliction*

5. And thus the Scripture is fulfilled, "Blessed are they that mourn, for they shall be comforted." For it is easy to believe, that though sorrow may precede this witness of

God's Spirit with our spirit (indeed *must*, in some degree, while we groan under fear, and a sense of the wrath of God abiding on us); yet, as soon as any man feels it in himself, his "sorrow is turned into joy." Whatever his pain may have been before; yet, as soon as that "hour has come, he remembers the anguish no more, for joy" that he is born of God. It may be, many of *you* have now sorrow, because you are "aliens from the commonwealth of Israel"; because you are conscious to yourselves that you do not have this Spirit; that you are "without hope and without God in the world."

But when the Comforter has come, "then your heart shall rejoice"; indeed, "your joy shall be full," and "that joy no man will take from you" (John 16:22). "We joy in God," you will say, "through our Lord Jesus Christ, by whom we have now received the atonement"; "by whom we have access into this grace," this state of grace, of favor, or reconciliation with God, "in which we stand, and rejoice in hope of the glory of God" (Rom. 5:2). "You," St. Peter says, whom God has "given new birth into a lively hope, are kept by the power of God unto salvation: in which you greatly rejoice, though now for a season, if need be, you are in heaviness through manifold temptations; that the trial of your faith may be found unto praise, and honor, and glory, at the appearing of Jesus Christ, in whom, though now you do not see him, you rejoice with joy unspeakable and full of glory" (see 1 Pet. 1:3–8).

Unspeakable indeed! It is not for the tongue of man to describe this joy in the Holy Spirit. It is "the hidden manna, which no man knows, save he who receives it." But this we know, it not only remains, but overflows, in the depth of affliction. "Are the consolations of God small" with his children, when all earthly comforts fail? Not so. But when sufferings most abound, the consolations of his Spirit do much more abound; so that the sons of God "laugh at destruction when it comes;" at want, pain, hell, and the grave; as knowing him who "has the keys of death and hell," and will shortly "cast them into the bottomless pit"; as hearing even now the great voice out of heaven, saying, "Behold, the tabernacle of God is with men, and he will dwell with them, and they shall be his people, and God himself shall be with them, and be their God. And God shall wipe away all tears from their eyes, and there shall be no more death, neither sorrow, nor crying, neither shall there be any more pain; for the former things have passed away" (Rev. 21:3–4).

## III. The New Birth Is Marked by Love

1. A third scriptural mark of those who are born of God, and the greatest of all, is love; even "the love of God shed abroad in their hearts by the Holy Spirit which is given unto them" (Rom. 5:5). "Because they are sons, God has sent forth the Spirit of his Son in their hearts, crying, Abba, Father!" (Gal. 4:6). By this Spirit, continually looking up to God as their reconciled and loving Father, they cry to him for their daily bread, for all things needful, whether for their souls or bodies. They continually pour out their hearts before him, knowing "they have the petitions which they ask of him" (1 John 5:15). Their delight is in him. He is the joy of their heart; their "shield," and their "exceeding great reward." The desire of their soul is toward him; it is their "meat and drink to do his will"; and they are "satisfied as with marrow and fatness, while their mouth praises him with joyful lips" (Ps. 63:5).

2. And, in this sense also, "everyone who loves the Father loves whoever has been born of him" (1 John 5:1 ESV). His spirit rejoices in God his Savior. He "loves the Lord Jesus Christ in sincerity." He is so "joined unto the Lord," as to be one spirit. His soul hangs upon him, and chooses him

as altogether lovely, "the chief among ten thousand." He knows, he feels what it means: "My beloved is mine, and I am his" (Song 2:16). "You are fairer than the children of men; full of grace are your lips, because God has anointed you for ever!" (Ps. 45:2).

## Love Bears the Fruit of Love for Our Neighbor

3. The necessary fruit of this love of God is the love of our neighbor; of every soul which God has made; not excluding our enemies; not excluding those who are now "despitefully using and persecuting us"—a love by which we love every man as ourselves; as we love our own souls. Moreover, our Lord has expressed it still more strongly, teaching us to "love one another even as he has loved us." Accordingly, the commandment written in the hearts of all those that love God, is no other than this, "As I have loved you, so love one another."

Now, "we perceive the love of God in this, that he laid down his life for us" (1 John 3:16). "We ought," then, as the Apostle justly infers, "to lay down our lives for the brethren." If we feel ourselves ready to do this, then we do truly love our neighbor. Then "we know that we have passed from death unto life, because we" thus "love the brethren" (1 John 3:14). "By this know we" that we are born of God, that we "dwell in him, and he in us, because he has given us of his" loving "Spirit" (1 John 4:13). For "love is of God and every one who" thus "loves is born of God, and knows God" (1 John 4:7).

4. But some may possibly ask, "Does not the Apostle say, 'This is the love of God, that we keep his commandments'?" (1 John 5:3). Indeed, and this is the love of our neighbor also, in the same sense as it is the love of God. But what would you infer from this? That the keeping of the outward commandments is all that is implied in loving God with all your heart, with all your mind, and soul, and strength, and in loving your

neighbor as yourself? That the love of God is not an affection of the soul, but merely an *outward service*? And that the love of our neighbor is not a disposition of heart, but barely a course of *outward works*? To mention so wild an interpretation of the Apostle's words is sufficiently to confute it.

The plain indisputable meaning of that text is—this is the sign or proof of the love of God, of our keeping the first and great commandment, to keep the rest of his commandments. For true love, if it is once shed abroad in our heart, will constrain us to do so; since, whoever loves God with all his heart, cannot but serve him with all his strength.

### Love Bears the Fruit of Obedience

5. A second fruit then of the love of God (so far as it can be distinguished from it) is universal obedience to him we love, and conformity to his will; obedience to all the commands of God, internal and external; obedience of the heart and of the life; in every temper, and in all manner of conversation. And one of the tempers most obviously implied in this, is the being "zealous of good works"; the hungering and thirsting to do good, in every possible kind, unto all men; the rejoicing to "spend and be spent for them," for every child of man; not looking for any recompense in this world, but only in the resurrection of the just.

## IV. What Is It to Be Born of God?

### Faith, Hope, and Love Mark the One Born of the Spirit of God

1. Thus I have plainly laid down those marks of the new birth that I find laid down in Scripture. Thus does God himself answer that weighty question: What is it to be born

of God? Such, if the appeal is made to the oracles of God, is "every one that is born of the Spirit." This it is, in the judgment of the Spirit of God, to be a son or a child of God: it is so to *believe* in God, through Christ, as "not to commit sin," and to enjoy at all times, and in all places, that "peace of God which passes all understanding." It is so to *hope* in God through the Son of his love, as to have not only the "testimony of a good conscience," but also the Spirit of God "bearing witness with your spirits, that you are the children of God"; from which cannot but spring the rejoicing in him, through whom you "have received the atonement." It is so to *love* God, who has thus loved you, as you never did love any creature: so that you are constrained to love all men as yourselves; with a love not only ever burning in your hearts, but flaming out in all your actions and conversations, and making your whole life one "labor of love," one continued obedience to those commands, "Be merciful, as God is merciful"; "Be holy, as I the Lord am holy"; "Be perfect, as your Father who is in heaven is perfect."

2. Who then are you that are *thus* born of God? You "know the things which are given to you of God." You know well that you are the children of God, and "can assure your hearts before him." And every one of you who has observed these words cannot but feel and know of a truth, whether at this hour (answer to God, and not to man!) you are thus a child of God or not.

The question is not, what you were made in baptism (do not evade); but, what are you now? Is the Spirit of adoption now in your heart? To your own heart let the appeal be made. I ask not, whether you *were* born of water and of the Spirit; but are you *now* the temple of the Holy Spirit which dwells in you? I allow you were "circumcised with the circumcision of Christ" (as St. Paul emphatically terms baptism); but does the Spirit of Christ and of glory *now* rest upon you? Otherwise "your circumcision has become uncircumcision."

## Baptism and the New Birth Are Not One in the Same

3. Say not then in your heart, "I *was once* baptized, therefore I *am now* a child of God." Alas, that consequence will by no means hold. How many are the baptized gluttons and drunkards, the baptized liars and common swearers, the baptized revilers and evil-speakers, the baptized fornicators, thieves, extortionists? What do you think? Are these now the children of God? Truly, I say unto you, whoever you are, unto whom any one of the preceding characters belongs, "You are of your father the devil, and you do the works of your father." Unto you I call, in the name of him whom you crucify afresh, and in his words to your circumcised predecessors, "You serpents, you generation of vipers, how can you escape the damnation of hell?"

4. How, indeed, unless you are born again! For you are now dead in trespasses and sins. To say, then, that you cannot be born again, that there is no new birth but in baptism, is to seal you all under damnation, to consign you to hell, without help, without hope. And perhaps some may think this just and right. In their zeal for the Lord of hosts, they may say, "Indeed, cut off the sinners, the Amalekites! Let these Gibeonites be utterly destroyed! They deserve no less." No, nor I, nor you. Your desert and mine, as well as theirs, is hell; and it is mere mercy, free, undeserved mercy, that *we* are not now in unquenchable fire.

You will say, "But we are washed"; we were born again "of water and of the Spirit." So *were* they: this, therefore, hinders not at all, but that you may *now* be even as they. Do you not know that "what is highly esteemed of men is an abomination in the sight of God"? Come forth, you "saints of the world," you that are honored of men, and see who will cast the first stone at them, at these wretches not fit to live upon the earth, these common harlots, adulterers, murderers. Only learn first what that means, "He who hates his brother is a murderer" (1 John 3:15). "He who looks on a woman, to lust after her, has committed adultery with her already in his heart" (Matt. 5:28). "You adulterers and adulteresses, do you not know that the friendship of the world is enmity with God?" (James 4:4).

## You Must Be Born Again

5. "Truly, Truly, I say unto you, you" also "must be born again." "Unless you" also "are born again, you cannot see the kingdom of God." Lean no more on the staff of that broken reed—that ye *were* born again in baptism. Who denies that you were then made children of God, and heirs of the kingdom of heaven? But, notwithstanding this, you are now children of the devil. Therefore you must be born again. And let not Satan put it into your heart to cavil at a word, when the thing is clear. You have heard what are the marks of the children of God: all you who do not have them on your souls, baptized or unbaptized, must receive them, or without doubt you will perish everlastingly. And if you have been baptized, your only hope is this, that those who were made the children of God by baptism, but are now the children of the devil, may yet again receive "power to become the sons of God"; that they may receive again what they have lost, even the "Spirit of adoption, crying in their hearts, Abba, Father!"

Amen, Lord Jesus! May every one who prepares his heart yet again to seek your face, receive again that Spirit of adoption, and cry out, "Abba, Father!" Let him now again have power so to believe in your name as to become a child of God; as to know and feel he has "redemption in your blood, even the forgiveness of sins"; and that he "cannot commit sin, because he is born of God." Let him be now "born again unto a living hope," so as to "purify himself as you are pure"; and "because he is a son," let the Spirit of love and of glory rest upon him, cleansing him "from all filthiness of flesh and spirit," and teaching him to "perfect holiness in the fear of God!"

# SIX

# ON SIN IN BELIEVERS

## 1763

*If any man is in Christ, he is a new creature.*
—2 Corinthians 5:17

## I. Does Sin Remain in One Who Believes in Christ?

1. Is there then sin in him who is in Christ? Does sin *remain* in one who believes in him? Is there any sin in those that are born of God, or are they wholly delivered from it? Let no one imagine this to be a question of mere curiosity; or that it is of little importance whether it is determined one way or the other. Rather it is a point of the utmost importance to every serious Christian; the resolving of which very nearly concerns both his present and eternal happiness.

### The Church's Historical Understanding of Remaining Sin

2. And yet I do not know that ever it was controverted in the primitive Church. Indeed there was no room for

disputing concerning it, as all Christians were agreed. And so far as I have observed, the whole body of ancient Christians, who have left us anything in writing, declare with one voice, that even believers in Christ, till they are "strong in the Lord, and in the power of his might," have need to "wrestle with flesh and blood," with an evil nature, as well as "with principalities and powers."

3. And in this our own Church (as indeed in most points) exactly copies after the primitive; declaring in her Ninth Article, "Original sin is the corruption of the nature of every man, whereby man is in his own nature inclined to evil, so that the flesh lusts contrary to the Spirit. And this infection of nature does remain, indeed, in those who are regenerated; whereby *the lust of the flesh*, called in Greek φρόνημα σάρκος, is not subject to the law of God. And although there is no condemnation for those who believe, yet this lust has of itself the nature of sin."

4. The same testimony is given by all other Churches; not only by the Greek and Roman Church, but by every Reformed Church in Europe, of whatever denomination. Indeed some of these seem to carry the thing too far; so describing the corruption of heart in a believer, as scarce to allow that he has dominion over it, but rather is in bondage to it; and, by this means, they leave hardly any distinction between a believer and an unbeliever.

## Alternative Interpretations of Remaining Sin

5. To avoid this extreme, many well-meaning men, particularly those under the direction of the late Count Zinzendorf, ran into another; affirming, that "all true believers are not only saved from the *dominion* of sin, but from the *being* of inward as well as outward sin, so that it no

longer *remains* in them." And from them, about twenty years ago, many of our countrymen imbibed the same opinion, that even the corruption of nature *is no more,* in those who believe in Christ.

6. It is true that, when the Germans were pressed upon this head, they soon allowed (many of them at least), that "sin did still remain *in the flesh,* but not *in the heart* of a believer"; and, after a time, when the absurdity of this was shown, they fairly gave up the point; allowing that sin did still remain, though not reign, in him who is born of God.

7. But the English, who had received it from them (some directly, some at second or third hand), were not so easily prevailed upon to part with a favorite opinion; and even when the generality of them were convinced it was utterly indefensible, a few could not be persuaded to give it up, but maintain it to this day.

## II. Is a Justified Man Free from *Both* Inward and Outward Sin?

1. For the sake of these who really fear God, and desire to know "the truth as it is in Jesus," it may not be amiss to consider the point with calmness and impartiality. In doing this, I use indifferently the words, *regenerate, justified,* or *believers;* since, though they do not have precisely the same meaning (the first implying an inward, actual change; the second, a relative one; and the third, the means by which both the one and the other are wrought), yet they come to one and the same thing; as everyone who believes, is both justified and born of God.

2. By sin, I here understand *inward sin*; any sinful temper, passion, or affection; such as pride, self-will, love of the

world, in any kind or degree; such as lust, anger, peevishness; any disposition contrary to the mind which was in Christ.

3. The question is not concerning *outward sin;* whether a child of God *commits sin* or no. We all agree and earnestly maintain, "He who commits sin is of the devil." We agree, "Whoever is born of God does not commit sin." Neither do we now inquire whether inward sin will *always* remain in the children of God; whether sin will continue in the soul as long as it continues in the body; nor yet do we inquire whether a justified person may *relapse* either into inward or outward sin; but simply this: Is a justified or regenerate man freed from *all sin* as soon as he is justified? Is there then no sin in his heart—nor ever after, unless he should fall from grace?

4. We allow that the state of a justified person is inexpressibly great and glorious. He is born again, "not of blood, nor of the flesh, nor of the will of man, but of God." He is a child of God, a member of Christ, an heir of the kingdom of heaven. "The peace of God, which passes all understanding, keeps his heart and mind in Christ Jesus." His very body is a "temple of the Holy Spirit," and a "habitation of God through the Spirit."

He is "created anew in Christ Jesus": he is *washed,* he is *sanctified.* His heart is purified by faith; he is cleansed "from the corruption that is in the world"; "the love of God is shed abroad in his heart by the Holy Spirit which is given unto him." And so long as he "walks in love" (which he may always do), he worships God in spirit and in truth. He keeps the commandments of God, and does those things that are pleasing in his sight; so exercising himself as to "have a conscience void of offense, toward God and toward man." And he has power over both outward and inward sin, even from the moment he is justified.

# III. Is the Believer's Heart Freed from All Sin?

## No, It Is Contrary to the Word of God

1. "But was he not then freed from all sin, so that there is no sin in his heart?" I cannot say this; I cannot believe it, because St. Paul says the contrary. He is speaking to believers, and describing the state of believers in general, when he says, "The flesh lusts against the Spirit, and the Spirit against the flesh: these are contrary the one to the other" (Gal. 5:17). Nothing can be more express. The Apostle here directly affirms that the flesh, evil nature, opposes the Spirit, even in believers; that even in the regenerate there are two principles, "contrary the one to the other."

2. Again, when he writes to the believers at Corinth, to those who were sanctified in Christ Jesus (1 Cor. 1:2), he says, "I, brethren, could not speak to you as to spiritual people but as to carnal, as to babes in Christ. You are still carnal. For where there are envy, strife, and divisions among you, are you not carnal?" (1 Cor. 3:1, 3 NKJV). Now here the Apostle speaks to those who were unquestionably believers—who, in the same breath, he styles his brethren in Christ—as being still, in a measure, carnal. He affirms, there was envying (an evil temper), occasioning strife among them, and yet does not give the least intimation that they had lost their faith. Moreover, he manifestly declares they had not; for then they would not have been babes in Christ. And (what is most remarkable of all) he speaks of being carnal, and babes in Christ, as one and the same thing; plainly showing that every believer is (in a degree) carnal, while he is only a babe in Christ.

3. Indeed this grand point, that there are two contrary principles in believers—nature and grace, the flesh and the Spirit, runs through all the Epistles of St. Paul, indeed, through all the Holy Scriptures; almost all the directions

and exhortations in them are founded on this supposition; pointing at wrong tempers or practices in those who are, notwithstanding, acknowledged by the inspired writers to be believers. And they are continually exhorted to fight with and conquer these, by the power of the faith that was in them.

4. And who can doubt, but there was faith in the angel of the church of Ephesus, when our Lord said to him, "I know your works, and your labor, and your patience: you have patience, and for my name's sake have labored, and have not fainted" (Rev. 2:2–4). But was there, meantime, no sin in his heart? Indeed, or Christ would not have added, "Nevertheless, I have something against you, because you have left your first love." This was real sin which God saw in his heart; of which, accordingly, he is exhorted to *repent;* and yet we have no authority to say, that even then he had no faith.

5. Moreover, the angel of the church at Pergamos, also, is exhorted to *repent,* which implies sin, though our Lord expressly says, "You have not denied my faith" (Rev. 2:13, 16). And to the angel of the church in Sardis, he says, "Strengthen the things which remain, that are ready to die." The good which remained was *ready to die,* but was not actually dead (Rev. 3:2). So there was still a spark of faith even in him; which he is accordingly commanded to *hold fast* (Rev. 3:3).

6. Once more, when the Apostle exhorts believers to "cleanse themselves from all filthiness of flesh and spirit" (2 Cor. 7:1), he plainly teaches that those believers were not yet cleansed from it. Will you answer, "He who abstains from all appearance of evil, does *ipso facto* cleanse himself from all filthiness?" Not in any way. For instance: A man reviles me; I feel resentment, which is filthiness of spirit; yet I do not say a word. Here I "abstain from all appearance of evil"; but this does not cleanse me from that filthiness of spirit, as I experience to my sorrow.

## No, It Is Contrary to the Experience of God's Children

7. And as this position, "There is no sin in a believer, no carnal mind, no bent to backsliding," is thus contrary to the word of God, so it is to the experience of his children. These continually feel a heart bent to backsliding; a natural tendency to evil; a proneness to depart from God, and cleave to the things of earth. They are daily sensible of sin remaining in their heart—pride, self-will, unbelief—and of sin cleaving to all they speak and do, even their best actions and holiest duties.

Yet at the same time they "know that they are of God"; they cannot doubt of it for a moment. They feel his Spirit clearly "witnessing with their spirit, that they are the children of God." They "rejoice in God through Christ Jesus, by whom they have now received the atonement." So that they are equally assured, that sin is in them, and that "Christ is in them, the hope of glory."

8. "But can Christ be in the same heart where sin is?" Undoubtedly he can; otherwise it never could be saved from it. Where the sickness is, there is the Physician,

*Carrying on his work within,*
*Striving till he cast out sin.*

Christ indeed cannot *reign,* where sin *reigns;* neither will he *dwell* where any sin is *allowed.* But he *is* and *dwells* in the heart of every believer, who is *fighting against* all sin; although it is not yet purified, according to the purification of the sanctuary.

## No, It Is an Utterly New Doctrine

9. It has been observed before, that the opposite doctrine—that there is no sin in believers—is quite new in the church of Christ; that it was never heard of for

seventeen hundred years; never till it was discovered by Count Zinzendorf. I do not remember to have seen the least intimation of it, either in any ancient or modern writer; unless perhaps in some of the wild, ranting Antinomians. And these likewise say and unsay, acknowledging there is sin *in their flesh,* although no *sin in their heart.* But whatever doctrine is *new* must be wrong; for the *old* religion is the only *true one;* and no doctrine can be right, unless it is the very same "which was from the beginning."

## No, It Brings About the Most Fatal Consequences

10. One argument more against this new, unscriptural doctrine may be drawn from the dreadful consequences of it. One says, "I felt anger today." Must I reply, "Then you have no faith?" Another says, "I know what you advise is good, but my will is quite averse to it." Must I tell him, "Then you are an unbeliever, under the wrath and the curse of God?" What will be the natural consequence of this? Why, if he believes what I say, his soul will not only be grieved and wounded, but perhaps utterly destroyed; inasmuch as he will "cast away" that "confidence which has great recompense of reward"; and having cast away his shield, how shall he "quench the fiery darts of the wicked one?" How shall he overcome the world—seeing "this is the victory that overcomes the world, even our faith?" He stands disarmed in the midst of his enemies, open to all their assaults. What wonder then, if he should be utterly overthrown; if they take him captive at their will; indeed, if he should fall from one wickedness to another, and never see good any more?

I cannot, therefore, by any means receive this assertion, that there is no sin in a believer from the moment he is justified; first, because it is contrary to the whole tenor of Scripture; secondly, because it is contrary to the experience of the children of God; thirdly, because it is absolutely new, never heard of in the world till yesterday; and lastly, because it is naturally attended with the most fatal consequences; not only grieving those whom God has not grieved, but perhaps dragging them into everlasting perdition.

## IV. Arguments That Claim There Is No Sin in Believers

### That a Man Cannot Be at the Same Time Holy and Unholy

1. However, let us give a fair hearing to the chief arguments of those who endeavor to support it. And it is, first, from Scripture they attempt to prove that there is no sin in a believer. They argue thus: "The Scripture says: every believer is born of God, is clean, is holy, is sanctified, is pure in heart, has a new heart, is a temple of the Holy Spirit. Now, as 'that which is born of the flesh is flesh,' is altogether evil, so 'that which is born of the Spirit is spirit,' is altogether good. Again, a man cannot be clean, sanctified, holy, and at the same time unclean, unsanctified, unholy. He cannot be pure and impure, or have a new and an old heart together. Neither can his soul be unholy, while it is a temple of the Holy Spirit."

I have put this objection as strongly as possible, that its full weight may appear. Let us now examine it, part by part. And, first, "that which is born of the Spirit is spirit, is altogether good." I allow the text, but not the comment. For the text affirms this, and no more: that every man who is "born of the Spirit," is a spiritual man. He is so, but so he may be, and yet not be altogether spiritual. The Christians at Corinth were spiritual men; or else they had been no Christians at all; and yet they were not altogether spiritual; they were still, in part, carnal—"but they were fallen from grace." St. Paul says, no, they were even then babes in Christ.

Secondly, "but a man cannot be clean, sanctified, holy, and at the same time unclean, unsanctified, unholy." Indeed he may. So the Corinthians were. "You are washed," says the Apostle, "you are sanctified"—namely, cleansed from "fornication, idolatry, drunkenness," and all other outward sin (1 Cor. 6:9–11)—and yet at the same time, in another sense of the word, they were unsanctified; they were not washed, not inwardly cleansed from envy, evil surmising, partiality.

"But sure, they did not have a new heart and an old heart together." It is most sure they did, for at that very time, their hearts were *truly,* yet not *entirely,* renewed. Their carnal mind was nailed to the cross; yet it was not wholly destroyed.

"But could they be unholy while they were 'temples of the Holy Spirit'?" Yes, that they were temples of the Holy Spirit, is certain (1 Cor. 6:19); and it is equally certain they were, in some degree, carnal, that is, unholy.

## *That He Who Is in Christ Is Altogether a New Creation*

2. "However, there is one Scripture more which will put the matter out of question: 'If any man is' a believer 'in Christ, he is a new creature. Old things are passed away; behold, all things have become new' (2 Cor. 5:17). Now certainly a man cannot be a new creature and an old creature at once." Yes, he may: he may be partly renewed, which was the very case with those at Corinth. They were doubtless "renewed in the spirit of their mind," or they could not have been so much as "babes in Christ." Yet they did not have the whole mind that was in Christ, for they envied one another.

"But it is said expressly, 'Old things are passed away: all things have become new.'" But we must not so interpret the

Apostle's words, as to make him contradict himself. And if we will make him consistent with himself, the plain meaning of the words is this: his old judgment concerning justification, holiness, happiness, indeed concerning the things of God in general, have now passed away; so have his old desires, designs, affections, tempers, and conversation. All these have undeniably become new, greatly changed from what they were; and yet, though they are new, they are not wholly new. Still he feels, to his sorrow and shame, remains of the old man, too manifest taints of his former tempers and affections, though they cannot gain any advantage over him, as long as he watches unto prayer.

3. This whole argument, "If he is clean, he is clean"; "If he is holy, he is holy" (and twenty more expressions of the same kind may easily be heaped together); is really no better than playing upon words: it is the fallacy of arguing from a *particular to a general;* of inferring a general conclusion from particular premises. Propose the entire sentence, and it runs thus: "If he is holy *at all,* he is holy *altogether.*" That does not follow: every babe in Christ is holy, and yet not altogether so. He is saved from sin; yet not entirely: it *remains,* though it does not *reign.*

If you think it does not *remain* (in babes at least, whatever be the case with young men, or fathers), you certainly have not considered the height, and depth, and length, and breadth of the law of God (even the law of love, laid down by St. Paul in the thirteenth of Corinthians); and that *every anomia*, disconformity to, or deviation from, this law *is sin.* Now, is there no disconformity to this in the heart or life of a believer? What may be in an adult Christian, is another question; but what a stranger must he be to human nature, who can possibly imagine that this is the case with every babe in Christ!

## That He Who Walks after the Spirit Is Delivered from the Being of Sin

4. "But believers walk after the Spirit (Rom. 8:1),* and the Spirit of God dwells in them; consequently, they are delivered from the guilt, the power, or, in one word, the *being* of sin." These are coupled together, as if they were the same thing. But they are not the same thing. The *guilt* is one thing, the *power* another, and the *being* yet another. That believers are delivered from the *guilt* and *power* of sin we allow; that they are delivered from the *being* of it we deny. Nor does it in any way follow from these texts. A man may have the Spirit of God dwelling in him, and may "walk after the Spirit," though he still feels "the flesh lusting against the Spirit."

5. "But the 'church is the body of Christ' (Col. 1:24). This implies, that its members are washed from all filthiness; otherwise it will follow that Christ and Belial are incorporated with each other." Moreover, it will not follow from this: "Those who are the mystical body of Christ, still feel the flesh lusting against the Spirit," that Christ has any fellowship with the devil or with that sin which he enables them to resist and overcome.

6. "But have not Christians 'come to the heavenly Jerusalem,' where 'nothing defiled can enter'?" (Heb. 12:22). Yes, "and to an innumerable company of angels, and to the spirits of just men made perfect." That is,

---

*Wesley's original edition notes at this point that the thrust of his argument in the subsequent paragraphs of the sermon is intended to answer an essay published in the *Christian Magazine* with which he disagrees, specifically around the issue of whether the "being" of sin remains in the believer.

*Earth and heaven all agree;*
*All is one great family.*

And they are likewise holy and undefiled, while they "walk after the Spirit"; although sensible there is another principle in them, and that "these are contrary to each other."

7. "But Christians are reconciled to God. Now this could not be, if any of the carnal mind remained; for this is enmity against God. Consequently, no reconciliation can be effected, but by its total destruction." We are "reconciled to God through the blood of the cross." And in that moment the φρόνημα σάρκος, the corruption of nature, which is enmity with God, is put under our feet; the flesh has no more dominion over us. But it still *exists;* and it is still in its nature enmity with God, lusting against his Spirit.

8. "But 'they who are Christ's have crucified the flesh, with its affections and lusts'" (Gal. 5:24). They have; yet it remains in them still, and often struggles to break from the cross. "Indeed, but they have 'put off the old man with his deeds'" (Col. 3:9). They have; and, in the sense above described, "old things are passed away; all things have become new." A hundred texts may be cited to the same effect; and they will all admit of the same answer.

"But, to say all in one word, 'Christ gave himself for the Church, that it might be holy and without blemish'" (Eph. 5:25, 27). And so it will be in the end; but it never was yet, from the beginning to this day.

9. "But let experience speak: all who are justified do at that time find an absolute freedom from all sin." That I doubt; but, if they do, do they find it ever after? Otherwise you gain nothing.

"If they do not, it is their own fault." That remains to be proved.

## *That Sin Cannot Exist Where It Does Not Reign*

10. "But, in the very nature of things, can a man have pride in him, and not be proud; anger, and yet not be angry?" A man may have *pride* in him, may think of himself in some particulars above what he ought to think (and so be proud in that particular), and yet not be a proud man in his general character. He may have *anger* in him, indeed, and a strong propensity to furious anger, without *giving way* to it.

"But can anger and pride be in that heart, where *only* meekness and humility are felt?" No, but *some* pride and anger may be in that heart, where there is much humility and meekness.

"It does not avail to say these tempers are there, but they do not *reign:* for sin cannot, in any kind or degree, exist where it does not reign; for *guilt* and *power* are essential properties of sin. Therefore, where one of them is, all must be." Strange indeed! "Sin cannot, in any kind or degree, *exist* where it does not *reign?*" This is absolutely contrary to all experience, all Scripture, all common sense. Resentment of an affront is sin; it is *anomia,* disconformity to the law of love. This has existed in me a thousand times. Yet it did not, and does not, *reign.*

"But *guilt* and *power* are essential properties of sin; therefore where one is, all must be." No, in the instance before us, if the resentment I feel is not yielded to, even for a moment, there is no guilt at all, no condemnation from God upon that account. And in this case, it has no *power:* though it "lusts against the Spirit," it cannot prevail. Here, therefore, as in ten thousand instances, there is *sin* without either *guilt* or *power.*

11. "But the assumption of sin in a believer is pregnant with everything frightful and discouraging. It implies the contending with a power that has the possession of our strength; maintains his usurpation of our hearts; and there

prosecutes the war in defiance of our Redeemer." Not so. The assumption of sin in us does not imply that it has the possession of our strength; no more than a man crucified has the possession of those that crucify him. As little does it imply, that "sin maintains its usurpation of our hearts." The usurper is dethroned. He remains indeed where he once reigned; but remains *in chains*. So that he does, in some sense, "continue the war," yet he grows weaker and weaker; while the believer goes on from strength to strength, conquering and to conquer.

## That Those with Sin Remaining in Them Are Enslaved to Sin

12. "I am not satisfied yet: he who has sin in him, is a slave to sin. Therefore you suppose a man to be justified, while he is a slave to sin. Now, if you allow that men may be justified while they have pride, anger, or unbelief in them; moreover, if you assert these are (at least for a time) in all who are justified; what wonder that we have so many proud, angry, unbelieving believers!" I do not suppose any man who is justified is a slave to sin; yet I do suppose sin remains (at least for a time) in all who are justified.

"But, if sin remains in a believer, he is a sinful man: if pride, for instance, then he is proud; if self-will, then he is self-willed; if unbelief, then he is an unbeliever; consequently, no believer at all. How then does he differ from unbelievers, from unregenerate men?" This is still mere playing upon words. It means no more than, if there is sin, pride, self-will in him, then there is sin, pride, self-will. And this nobody can deny. In that sense then he is proud, or self-willed. But he is not proud or self-willed in the same sense that unbelievers are; that is, *governed* by pride or self-will. In this he differs from unregenerate men. They *obey* sin; he does not. Flesh is in them both. But they "walk after the flesh"; he "walks after the Spirit."

"But how can *unbelief* be in a believer?" That word has two meanings. It means either no faith, or little faith; either the *absence* of faith or the *weakness* of it. In the former sense, unbelief is not in a believer; in the latter, it is in all babes. Their faith is commonly mixed with doubt or fear; that is, in the latter sense, with unbelief. "Why are you fearful," says our Lord, "O you of little faith?" Again, "O you of little faith, why did you doubt?" You see, here was *unbelief* in *believers;* little faith and much unbelief.

### *That the Doctrine of Sin in Believers Encourages Men to Sin*

13. "But this doctrine, that sin remains in a believer; that a man may be in the favor of God, while he has sin in his heart; certainly tends to encourage men in sin." Understand the proposition right, and no such consequence follows. A man may be in God's favor though he feel sin; but not if he *yields* to it. *Having sin* does not forfeit the favor of God; *giving way to sin* does. Though the flesh in you "lust against the Spirit," you may still be a child of God; but if you "walk after the flesh," you are a child of the devil. Now this doctrine does not encourage to *obey* sin, but to resist it with all our might.

## V. Two Contrary Principles

1. The sum of all is this: there are in every person, even after he is justified, two contrary principles, nature and grace, termed by St. Paul the *flesh* and the *Spirit.* Hence, although even babes in Christ are *sanctified,* yet it is only in part. In a

degree, according to the measure of their faith, they are spiritual; yet, in a degree they are carnal. Accordingly, believers are continually exhorted to watch against the flesh, as well as the world and the devil. And to this agrees the constant experience of the children of God. While they feel this witness in themselves, they feel a will not wholly resigned to the will of God. They know they are in him; and yet find a heart ready to depart from him, a proneness to evil in many instances, and a backwardness to that which is good.

The contrary doctrine is wholly new; never heard of in the church of Christ, from the time of his coming into the world, till the time of Count Zinzendorf; and it is attended with the most fatal consequences. It cuts off all watching against our evil nature, against the Delilah whom we are told is gone, though she is still lying in our bosom. It tears away the shield of weak believers, deprives them of their faith and so leaves them exposed to all the assaults of the world, the flesh, and the devil.

2. Let us, therefore, hold fast the sound doctrine "once delivered to the saints," and delivered down by them with the written word to all succeeding generations: that although we are renewed, cleansed, purified, sanctified, the moment we truly believe in Christ, yet we are not then renewed, cleansed, purified *altogether*; but the flesh, the evil nature, still *remains* (though subdued) and wars against the Spirit.

So much the more let us use all diligence in "fighting the good fight of faith." So much the more earnestly let us "watch and pray" against the enemy within. The more carefully let us take to ourselves, and "put on, the whole armor of God"; that, although "we wrestle" both "with flesh and blood, and with the principalities, and with powers, and wicked spirits in high places," we may be able to withstand in the evil day, and having done all, to stand.

# SEVEN

# The Repentance of Believers

## 1767

*"Repent, and believe the gospel."*

—Mark 1:15

## Introduction

1. It is generally supposed that repentance and faith are only the gate of religion; that they are necessary only at the beginning of our Christian course, when we are setting out in the way to the kingdom. And this may seem to be confirmed by the great Apostle, where, exhorting the Hebrew Christians to "go on to perfection," he teaches them to *leave* these first "principles of the doctrine of Christ"; "not laying again the foundation of repentance from dead works, and of faith towards God"; which must at least mean, that they should comparatively leave these, that at first took up all

their thoughts, in order to "press forward toward the prize of the high calling of God in Christ Jesus."

2. And this is undoubtedly true, that there is a repentance and a faith, which are, more especially, necessary at the beginning: a repentance, which is a conviction of our utter sinfulness, and guiltiness, and helplessness; and which precedes our receiving that kingdom of God which, our Lord observes, is "within us"; and a faith, by which we receive that kingdom, even "righteousness, and peace, and joy in the Holy Spirit."

3. But, notwithstanding this, there is also a repentance and a faith (taking the words in another sense, a sense not quite the same, nor yet entirely different) which are requisite *after* we have "believed the gospel"; indeed, and in every subsequent stage of our Christian course, or we cannot "run the race which is set before us." And this repentance and faith are full as necessary, in order to our *continuance* and *growth* in grace, as the former faith and repentance were, in order to our *entering* into the kingdom of God. But in what sense are we to repent and believe, after we are justified? This is an important question, and worthy of being considered with the utmost attention.

## I. In What Sense Are We to Repent After We Are Justified?

And, first, in what sense are we to repent?

### Sin Does Not Reign, but It Does Remain

1. Repentance frequently means an inward change, a change of mind from sin to holiness. But we now speak of it in a quite different sense, as it is one kind of self-knowledge,

the knowing ourselves to be sinners, indeed, guilty, helpless sinners, even though we know we are children of God.

2. Indeed when we first know this; when we first find the redemption in the blood of Jesus; when the love of God is first shed abroad in our hearts, and his kingdom set up therein; it is natural to suppose that we are no longer sinners, that all our sins are not only covered but destroyed. As we do not then feel any evil in our hearts, we readily imagine none is there.

Moreover, some well-meaning men have imagined this not only at that time, but ever after; having persuaded themselves, that when they were justified, they were entirely sanctified: indeed, they have laid it down as a general rule, in spite of Scripture, reason, and experience. These sincerely believe, and earnestly maintain, that all sin is destroyed when we are justified; and that there is no sin in the heart of a believer; but that it is altogether clean from that moment. But though we readily acknowledge, "he who believes is born of God," and "he who is born of God does not commit sin"; yet we cannot allow that he does not *feel* it from within: it does not *reign*, but it does remain. And a conviction of the sin that *remains* in our heart is one great branch of the repentance of which we are now speaking.

## Believers Repent of the Sin Remaining in their Hearts

3. For it is seldom long before he who imagined all sin was gone, feels there is still *pride* in his heart. He is convinced both that in many respects he has thought of himself more highly than he ought to think, and that he has taken to himself the praise of something he had received, and gloried in it as though he had not received it; and yet he knows he is in the favor of God. He cannot, and ought not to "cast away

his confidence." "The Spirit" still "witnesses with" his "spirit, that he is a child of God."

4. Nor is it long before he feels *self-will* in his heart; even a will contrary to the will of God. A will every man must inevitably have, as long as he has an understanding. This is an essential part of human nature, indeed of the nature of every intelligent being. Our blessed Lord himself had a will as a man, otherwise he had not been a man. But his human will was invariably subject to the will of his Father. At all times, and on all occasions, even in the deepest affliction, he could say, "Not as I will, but as you will."

But this is not the case at all times, even with a true believer in Christ. He frequently finds his will more or less exalting itself against the will of God. He wills something, because it is pleasing to nature, which is not pleasing to God; and he is averse from something, because it is painful to nature, which is the will of God concerning him. Indeed, suppose he continues in the faith, he fights against it with all his might: but this very thing implies that it really exists, and that he is conscious of it.

5. Now self-will, as well as pride, is a species of *idolatry* and both are directly contrary to the love of God. The same observation may be made concerning the *love of the world*. But this likewise even true believers are liable to feel in themselves; and every one of them does feel it, more or less, sooner or later, in one branch or another. It is true, when he first "passes from death unto life," he desires nothing more but God. He can truly say, "All my desire is unto you, and unto the remembrance of your name"; "Whom have I in heaven but you? And there is none upon earth that I desire beside you."

But it is not so always. In process of time he will feel again, though perhaps only for a few moments, either "the desire of the flesh," or "the desire of the eye," or "the pride of life." Moreover, if he does not continually watch and pray, he may find *lust* reviving; indeed, and thrusting sore at him that he may fall, till he has scarce any strength left in him. He may feel the assaults of *inordinate affection;* indeed, a strong propensity to "love the creature more than the Creator"; whether it be a child, a parent, a husband, or wife, or "the friend that is as his own soul." He may feel, in a thousand various ways, a desire of earthly things or pleasures. In the same proportion he will forget God, not seeking his happiness in him, and consequently being a "lover of pleasure more than a lover of God."

6. If he does not keep himself every moment, he will again feel *the desire of the eye;* the desire of gratifying his imagination with something great, or beautiful, or uncommon. In how many ways does this desire assault the soul! Perhaps with regard to the poorest trifles, such as dress, or furniture; things never designed to satisfy the appetite of an immortal spirit. Yet, how natural it is for us, even after we have "tasted of the powers of the world to come," to sink again into these foolish, low desires of things that perish in the using! How hard it is, even for those who know in whom they have believed, to conquer but one branch of the desire of the eye, *curiosity;* constantly to trample it under their feet; to desire nothing merely because it is new!

7. And how hard it is even for the children of God wholly to conquer the *pride of life*! St. John seems to mean by this nearly the same with what the world terms "the sense of honor." This is no other than a desire of, and delight in, "the honor that comes from men"; a desire and love of praise; and, which is always joined with it, a proportional *fear of dispraise.*

Nearly allied to this is *evil shame,* the being ashamed of that in which we ought to glory. And this is seldom divided from the *fear of man,* which brings a thousand snares upon the soul. Now where is he, even among those who seem strong in the faith, who does not find in himself a degree of all these evil tempers? So that even these are but in part "crucified to the world"; for the evil root still remains in their heart.

8. And do we not feel other tempers, which are as contrary to the love of our neighbor as these are to the love of God? The love of our neighbor "thinks no evil." Do we not find anything of the kind? Do we never find any *jealousies,* any *evil surmising,* any groundless or unreasonable suspicions? He who is clear in these respects, let him cast the first stone at his neighbor. Who does not sometimes feel other tempers or inward motions, which he knows are contrary to brotherly love?

If nothing of *malice, hatred,* or *bitterness,* is there no touch of *envy;* particularly toward those who enjoy some real or supposed good, which we desire, but cannot attain? Do we never find any degree of *resentment,* when we are injured or affronted; especially by those whom we peculiarly loved, and whom we had most labored to help or oblige? Does injustice or ingratitude never excite in us any desire of *revenge*, any desire of returning evil for evil, instead of "overcoming evil with good?" This also shows how much is still in our heart, which is contrary to the love of our neighbor.

9. *Covetousness,* in every kind and degree, is certainly as contrary to this as to the love of God; whether, *philargyri, the love of money,* which is too frequently "the root of all evil"; or *pleonexia,* literally, a desire of *having more,* or increasing in substance. And how few, even of the real children of God, are entirely free from both! Indeed one great man, Martin Luther, used to say, he "never had any covetousness in him" (not only in his converted state, but) "ever since he was born." But, if so, I would not scruple to say, he was the only man

born of a woman (except him that was God as well as man), who had not, who was born without it. Indeed, I believe, never was any one born of God, that lived any considerable time after, who did not feel more or less of it many times, especially in the latter sense. We may therefore set it down as an undoubted truth, that covetousness, together with pride, and self-will, and anger, remain in the hearts even of those who are justified.

10. It is their experiencing this, which has inclined so many serious persons to understand the latter part of the seventh chapter to the Romans, not of them that are "under the law," that are convinced of sin, which is undoubtedly the meaning of the Apostle, but of them that are "under grace"; that are "justified freely through the redemption that is in Christ." And it is most certain, they are thus far right: there does still *remain*, even in those who are justified, a *mind* which is in some measure *carnal* (so the Apostle tells even the believers at Corinth, "You are carnal"); a *heart bent to backsliding*, still ever ready to "depart from the living God"; a propensity to pride, self-will, anger, revenge, love of the world, indeed, and all evil; a root of bitterness, which, if the restraint were taken off for a moment, would instantly spring up; indeed, such a depth of corruption as, without clear light from God, we cannot possibly conceive. And a conviction of all this sin *remaining* in *their hearts* is the repentance that belongs to those who are justified.

## Believers Repent of Sin Cleaving to their Words and Intentions

11. But we should likewise be convinced, that as sin remains in our hearts, so it *cleaves* to all our words and actions. Indeed it is to be feared, that many of our words are more than mixed with sin; that they are sinful altogether; for

such undoubtedly is all *uncharitable conversation;* all which does not spring from brotherly love; all which does not agree with that golden rule, "What you wish that others should do to you, even so do unto them." Of this kind is all backbiting, all gossiping, all whispering, all evil-speaking, that is, repeating the faults of absent persons; for none would have others repeat his faults when he is absent.

Now how few are there, even among believers, who are in no degree guilty of this; who steadily observe the good old rule, "Of the dead and the absent, nothing but good!" And suppose they do, do they likewise abstain from *unprofitable conversation?* Yet all this is unquestionably sinful, and "grieves the Holy Spirit of God." Indeed, and "for every idle word that men shall speak, they shall give an account in the day of judgment."

12. But let it be supposed, that they continually "watch and pray," and so do "not enter into" this "temptation"; that they constantly set a watch before their mouth, and keep the door of their lips; suppose they exercise themselves in this, that *all* their "conversation may be in grace, seasoned with salt, and fit to minister grace to the hearers." Yet do they not daily slide into useless discourse, notwithstanding all their caution?

And even when they endeavor to speak for God, are their words pure, free from unholy mixtures? Do they find nothing wrong in their very *intention?* Do they speak merely to please God, and not partly to please themselves? Is it wholly to do the will of God, and not their own will also? Or, if they begin with a single eye, do they go on "looking unto Jesus," and talking with him all the time they are talking with their neighbor?

When they are reproving sin, do they feel no anger or unkind temper to the sinner? When they are instructing the ignorant, do they not find any pride, any self-preference?

When they are comforting the afflicted, or provoking one another to love and to good works, do they never perceive any inward self-commendation: "*Now you have spoken well*"—or any vanity, a desire that others should think so, and esteem them on the account? In some or all of these respects, how much sin cleaves to the best *conversation* even of believers! The conviction of which is another branch of the repentance that belongs to those who are justified.

## Believers Repent of Sin Cleaving to their Actions

13. And how much sin, if their conscience is thoroughly awake, may they find cleaving to *their actions* also! Indeed, are there not many of these, which, though they are such as the world would not condemn, yet cannot be commended, no, nor excused, if we judge by the Word of God? Are there not many of their actions that they themselves know are not to the glory of God? Many in which they did not even aim at this; which were not undertaken with an eye to God? And of those that were, are there not many in which their eye is not singly fixed on God; in which they are doing their own will, at least as much as his; and seeking to please themselves as much, if not more, than to please God?

And while they are endeavoring to do good to their neighbor, do they not feel wrong tempers of various kinds? Hence their good actions, so called, are far from being strictly such; being polluted with such a mixture of evil: such are their works of *mercy*. And is there not the same mixture in their works of *piety*? While they are hearing the word that is able to save their souls, do they not frequently find such thoughts as make them afraid lest it should turn to their condemnation, rather than their salvation? Is it not often the same case, while they are endeavoring to offer up their prayers to God, whether in public or private?

Moreover, while they are engaged in the most solemn service, even while they are at the table of the Lord, what manner of thoughts arises in them! Are not their hearts sometimes wandering to the ends of the earth; sometimes filled with such imaginations, as make them fear lest all their sacrifice should be an abomination to the Lord? So that they are now more ashamed of their best duties, than they were once of their worst sins.

14. Again: how many *sins of omission* are they chargeable with! We know the words of the Apostle: "To him who knows to do good, and does not do it, to him it is sin." But do they not know a thousand instances, in which they might have done good, to enemies, to strangers, to their brethren, either with regard to their bodies or their souls, and they did it not? How many omissions have they been guilty of, in their duty toward God! How many opportunities of communicating, of hearing his word, of public or private prayer, have they neglected! So great reason had even that holy man, Archbishop Usher, after all his labors for God, to cry out, almost with his dying breath, "Lord, forgive me my sins of omission!"

## Believers Repent of Inward Defects

15. But besides these outward omissions, may they not find in themselves *inward defects* without number? Defects of every kind: they have not the love, the fear, the confidence they ought to have, toward God. They have not the love which is due to their neighbor, to every child of man; no, nor even that which is due to their brethren, to every child of God, whether those that are at a distance from them, or those with whom they are immediately connected. They have no holy temper in the degree they ought; they are defective in everything—in a deep consciousness of which

they are ready to cry out, with M. De Renty, "I am a ground all overrun with thorns"; or, with Job, "I am vile; I abhor myself, and repent as in dust and ashes."

## Believers Repent of Their Guiltiness

16. A conviction of their *guiltiness* is another branch of that repentance which belongs to the children of God. But this is cautiously to be understood, and in a peculiar sense. For it is certain, "there is no condemnation to those who are in Christ Jesus," who believe in him, and, in the power of that faith, who "walk not after the flesh, but after the Spirit." Yet they can no more bear the *strict justice* of God now, than before they believed. This pronounces them to be still *worthy of death*, on all the preceding accounts. And it would absolutely condemn them to it, were it not for the atoning blood. Therefore they are thoroughly convinced, that they still *deserve* punishment, although it is hereby turned aside from them.

But here there are extremes on one hand and on the other, and few steer clear of them. Most men strike on one or the other, either thinking themselves condemned when they are not, or thinking they *deserve* to be acquitted. Indeed, the truth lies between: they still *deserve*, strictly speaking only the damnation of hell. But what they deserve does not come upon them, because they "have an Advocate with the Father." His life, and death, and intercession still interpose between them and condemnation.

## Believers Repent of Their Utter Helplessness

17. A conviction of their *utter helplessness* is yet another branch of this repentance. I mean hereby two things: first, that they are no more able now *of themselves* to think one good thought, to form one good desire, to speak one good

word, or do one good work, than before they were justified; that they have still no kind or degree of strength *of their own*; no power either to do good, or resist evil; no ability to conquer or even withstand the world, the devil, or their own evil nature. They can, it is certain, do all these things; but it is not by their own strength. They have power to overcome all these enemies; for "sin has no more dominion over them"; but it is not from nature, either in whole or in part; it is the *mere* gift of God: nor is it given all at once, as if they had a stock laid up for many years; but from moment to moment.

18. By this helplessness I mean, secondly, an absolute inability to deliver ourselves from that guiltiness or desert of punishment of which we are still conscious; indeed, and an inability to remove, by all the grace we have (to say nothing of our natural powers), either the pride, self-will, love of the world, anger, and general proneness to depart from God, which we experimentally know to *remain* in the heart, even of them that are regenerate; or the evil which, in spite of all our endeavors, cleaves to all our words and actions. Add to this, an utter inability wholly to avoid uncharitable and, much more, unprofitable, conversation: and an inability to avoid sins of omission, or to supply the numberless defects we are convinced of; especially the want of love, and other right tempers both to God and man.

### Nothing but a Gradual Work of God Will Drive Out These Enemies

19. If any man is not satisfied of this, if any believes that whoever is justified is able to remove these sins out of his heart and life, let him make the experiment. Let him try whether, by the grace he has already received, he can expel

pride, self-will, or inbred sin in general. Let him try whether he can cleanse his words and actions from all mixture of evil; whether he can avoid all uncharitable and unprofitable conversation, with all sins of omission; and, lastly, whether he can supply the numberless defects that he still finds in himself. Let him not be discouraged by one or two experiments, but repeat the trial again and again; and the longer he tries, the more deeply will he be convinced of his utter helplessness in all these respects.

20. Indeed this is so evident a truth, that well near all the children of God, scattered abroad, however they differ in other points, yet generally agree in this; that although we may "by the Spirit, mortify the deeds of the body," resist and conquer both outward and inward sin; although we may *weaken* our enemies day by day; yet we cannot *drive them out*. By all the grace that is given at justification we cannot uproot them. Though we watch and pray ever so much, we cannot wholly cleanse either our hearts or hands. Most sure we cannot, till it shall please our Lord to speak to our hearts again, to speak the second time, "Be clean"; and then only the leprosy is cleansed. Then only, the evil root, the carnal mind, is destroyed; and inbred sin subsists no more.

But if there be no such second change, if there be no instantaneous deliverance after justification, if there be *none but* a gradual work of God (that there is a gradual work none denies), then we must be content, as well as we can, to remain full of sin till death; and, if so, we must remain guilty till death, continually *deserving* punishment. For it is impossible the guilt, or desert of punishment, should be removed from us, as long as all this sin remains in our heart, and cleaves to our words and actions. Indeed, in rigorous justice, all we think, and speak, and act, continually increases it.

## II. In What Sense Are We to Believe the Gospel after We Are Justified?

1. In this sense we are to *repent*, after we are justified. And till we do so, we can go no farther. For, till we are sensible of our disease, it admits of no cure. But, supposing we do thus repent, then we are called to "believe the gospel."

### Believe He Is Able to Save

2. And this also is to be understood in a peculiar sense, different from that in which we believed in order to justification. Believe the glad tidings of great salvation, which God has prepared for all people. Believe that he who is "the brightness of his Father's glory, the express image of his person," is "able to save unto the uttermost all who come unto God through him." He is able to save you from all the sin that still remains in your heart. He is able to save you from all the sin that cleaves to all your words and actions. He is able to save you from sins of omission, and to supply whatever is wanting in you.

It is true, this is impossible with man; but with God-Man all things are possible. For what can be too hard for him who has "all power in heaven and in earth"? Indeed, his bare power to do this is not a sufficient foundation for our faith that he will do it, that he will thus exert his power, unless he has promised it. But this he has done: he has promised it over and over, in the strongest terms.

He has given us these "exceedingly great and precious promises," both in the Old and the New Testament. So we read in the law, in the most ancient part of the oracles of God, "The Lord your God will circumcise your heart, and the heart of your seed, to love the Lord your God with all

your heart, and with all your soul" (Deut. 30:6). So in the
Psalms, "He shall redeem Israel," the Israel of God, "from
all his sins." So in the Prophet, "Then will I sprinkle clean
water upon you, and you shall be clean: from all your filthiness, and from all your idols, I will cleanse you. And I will
put my Spirit within you, and you shall keep my judgments,
and do them. I will also save you from all your uncleanness"
(Ezek. 36:25, 27, 29).

So likewise in the New Testament, "Blessed be the Lord
God of Israel; for he has visited and redeemed his people, and
has raised up a horn of salvation for us . . . to perform the oath
which he swore to our father Abraham, that he would grant
to us, that we, being delivered out of the hands of our enemies,
should serve him without fear, in holiness and righteousness
before him, all the days of our life" (Luke 1:68–69, 72–75).

## Believe He Is Willing to Save

3. You have therefore good reason to believe, he is not
only able, but also willing to do this; to cleanse you from all
your filthiness of flesh and spirit; to "save you from all your
uncleanness." This is the thing which you now long for; this
is the faith which you now particularly need, namely, that
the Great Physician, the Lover of my soul, is willing to make
me clean.

But is he willing to do this tomorrow, or today? Let
him answer for himself: "Today, if you will hear" my "voice,
do not harden your hearts." If you put it off till tomorrow,
you harden your hearts; you refuse to hear his voice. Believe,
therefore, that he is willing to save you *today*. He is willing to
save you *now*. "Behold, now is the accepted time." He now
says, "Be clean!" Only believe, and you also will immediately
find, "all things are possible to him who believes."

## *Continue to Believe, from Faith to Faith*

4. Continue to believe in him who loved you, and gave himself for you; who bore all your sins in his own body on the tree; and who saves you from all condemnation, by his blood continually applied. Thus it is that we continue in a justified state. And when we go "from faith to faith," when we have faith to be cleansed from indwelling sin, to be saved from all our uncleanness, we are likewise saved from all that *guilt*, that *desert* of punishment, which we felt before. So that then we may say, not only,

> *Every moment, Lord, I want*
> *The merit of thy death;*

but, likewise, in the full assurance of faith,

> *Every moment, Lord, I have*
> *The merit of thy death!*

For, by that faith in his life, death, and intercession for us, renewed from moment to moment, we are every whit clean, and there is not only now no condemnation for us, but no such desert of punishment as was before, the Lord cleansing both our hearts and lives.

5. By the same faith we feel the power of Christ every moment resting upon us, by which alone we are what we are; by which we are enabled to continue in spiritual life, and without which, notwithstanding all our present holiness, we should be devils the next moment. But as long as we retain our faith in him, we "draw water out of the wells of salvation."

Leaning on our Beloved (even Christ in us, the hope of glory) who dwells in our hearts by faith, who likewise is ever interceding for us at the right hand of God, we receive help from him, to think, and speak, and act, what is acceptable in his sight. Thus does he "prevent" those who believe in all their "doings, and further them with his continual help"; so that all their designs, conversations, and actions are "begun, continued, and ended in him." Thus he does "cleanse the thoughts of their hearts, by the inspiration of his Holy Spirit, that they may perfectly love him, and worthily magnify his holy name."

## Repentance and Faith Answer Each Other

6. Thus it is, that in the children of God, repentance and faith exactly answer each other. By repentance, we feel the sin remaining in our hearts, and cleaving to our words and actions; by faith, we receive the power of God in Christ, purifying our hearts, and cleansing our hands. By repentance, we are still sensible that we deserve punishment for all our tempers, and words, and actions; by faith, we are conscious that our Advocate with the Father is continually pleading for us, and thereby continually turning aside all condemnation and punishment from us. By repentance we have an abiding conviction that there is no help in us; by faith we receive not only mercy, "but grace to help in" *every* time of need.

Repentance disclaims the very possibility of any other help; faith accepts all the help we stand in need of, from him who has all power in heaven and earth. Repentance says, "Without him I can do nothing"; faith says, "I can do all things through Christ strengthening me." Through him I can not only overcome, but also expel, all the enemies of my soul. Through him I can "love the Lord my God with all my heart, mind, soul, and strength"; indeed, and "walk in holiness and righteousness before him all the days of my life."

## III. Implications

1. From what has been said we may easily learn the mischievousness of that opinion, that we are *wholly* sanctified when we are justified; that our hearts are then cleansed from all sin. It is true, we are then delivered, as was observed before, from the dominion of outward sin; and, at the same time, the power of inward sin is so broken, that we need no longer follow, or be led by it. But it is by no means true, that inward sin is then totally destroyed; that the root of pride, self-will, anger, love of the world, is then taken out of the heart; or that the carnal mind and the heart bent to backsliding, are entirely uprooted. And to suppose the contrary is not, as some may think, an innocent harmless mistake.

No, it does immense harm. It entirely blocks up the way to any further change; for it is manifest, "they who are whole do not need a physician, but they who are sick." If, therefore, we think we are quite made whole already, there is no room to seek any further healing. On this supposition it is absurd to expect a further deliverance from sin, whether gradual or instantaneous.

### A Deep Conviction that We Are Not Whole

2. On the contrary, a deep conviction that *we are not yet whole*; that our hearts are not fully purified; that there is yet in us a "carnal mind," which is still in its nature "enmity against God"; that a whole body of sin remains in our heart, weakened indeed, but not destroyed; shows, beyond all possibility of doubt, the absolute necessity of a further change. We allow, that at the very moment of justification, we are *born again*. In that instant we experience that inward change from "darkness into marvelous light"; from the image of the brute and the devil, into the image of God; from the

earthly, sensual, devilish mind, to the mind which was in Christ Jesus.

But are we then *entirely* changed? Are we *wholly* transformed into the image of him who created us? Far from it: we still retain a depth of sin; and it is the consciousness of this that constrains us to groan, for a full deliverance, to him who is mighty to save. Thus it is, that those believers who are not convinced of the deep corruption of their hearts, or but slightly, and, as it were, notionally convinced, have little concern about *entire sanctification*. They may possibly hold the opinion that such a thing is to be, either at death, or some time they know not when, before it. But they have no great uneasiness for the want of it, and no great hunger or thirst after it. They cannot, until they know themselves better, until they repent in the sense above described, until God unveils the inbred monster's face, and shows them the real state of their souls. Then only, when they feel the burden, will they groan for deliverance from it. Then, and not till then, will they cry out, in the agony of their soul,

> *Break off the yoke of inbred sin,*
> *And fully set my spirit free!*
> *I cannot rest till pure within,*
> *Till I am wholly lost in Thee.*

## A Deep Conviction of Our Guilt

3. We may learn from this, secondly, that a deep conviction of our *demerit,* after we are accepted (which in one sense may be termed *guilt*), is absolutely necessary, in order to our seeing the true value of the atoning blood; in order to our feeling that we need this as much, after we are justified as ever we did before. Without this conviction, we cannot but account the blood of the covenant *as a common thing,* something of which

we have not now any great need, seeing all our past sins are blotted out. Indeed, but if both our hearts and lives are thus unclean, there is a kind of guilt which we are contracting every moment, and which, of consequence, would every moment expose us to fresh condemnation, but that

> *He ever lives above,*
> *For us to intercede,*
> *His all-atoning love,*
> *His precious blood, to plead.*

It is this repentance, and the faith intimately connected with it, which are expressed in those strong lines,

> *I sin in every breath I draw,*
> *Nor do Thy will, nor keep Thy law*
> *On earth, as angels do above:*
> *But still the fountain open stands,*
> *Washes my feet, my heart, my hands,*
> *Till I am perfected in love.*

## A Deep Conviction of Our Helplessness

4. We may observe, thirdly, a deep conviction of our utter *helplessness*, of our total inability to retain anything we have received, much more to deliver ourselves from the world of iniquity remaining both in our hearts and lives, teaches us truly to live upon Christ by faith, not only as our Priest, but as our King. By this we are brought to "magnify him," indeed, to "give him all the glory of his grace"—to "make him a whole Christ, an entire Savior; and truly to set the crown upon his head."

These excellent words, as they have frequently been used, have little or no meaning; but they are fulfilled in a strong and deep sense, when we thus, as it were, go out of ourselves in order to be swallowed up in him; when we sink into nothing, that he may be all in all. Then, his almighty grace having abolished "every high thing which exalted itself against him," every temper, and thought, and word, and work "is brought to the obedience of Christ."

# EIGHT

# The Good Steward

## 1768

*"Give an account of your stewardship, for you can no longer be steward."*

—Luke 16:2 NKJV

## Introduction

1. The relation that man bears to God, the creature to his Creator, is exhibited to us in the oracles of God under various representations. Considered as a sinner, a fallen creature, he is there represented as a debtor to his Creator. He is also frequently represented as a servant, which indeed is essential to him as a creature; so that this appellation is given to the Son of God when, in his state of humiliation, he "took upon himself the form of a servant, being made in the likeness of men."

2. But no character more exactly agrees with the present state of man, than that of a steward. Our blessed Lord frequently represents him as such; and there is a peculiar

propriety in the representation. It is only in one particular respect, namely, as he is a sinner, that he is styled a debtor; and when he is styled a servant, the appellation is general and indeterminate. But a steward is a servant of a particular kind; such a one as man is in all respects. This appellation is exactly expressive of his situation in the present world; specifying what kind of servant he is to God, and what kind of service his Divine Master expects from him.

It may be of use, then, to consider this point thoroughly, and to make our full improvement of it. In order to do this, let us, first, inquire in what respects we are now God's stewards. Let us, secondly, observe that when he requires our souls of us, we "can be no longer stewards." It will then only remain, as we may, in the third place, observe, to "give an account of our stewardship."

## I. In What Respects Are We Now God's Stewards?

1. First, we are to inquire, in what respects we are now God's stewards. We are now indebted to him for all we have; but although a debtor is obliged to return what he has received, yet until the time of payment comes, he is at liberty to use it as *he* pleases. It is not so with a steward; he is not at liberty to use what is lodged in his hands as he pleases, but as his master pleases. He has no right to dispose of anything that is in his hands, but according to the will of his lord. For he is not the proprietor of any of these things, but barely entrusted with them by another, and entrusted on this express condition, that he shall dispose of all as his master orders.

Now, this is exactly the case of every man, with relation to God. We are not at liberty to use what he has lodged in our hands as we please, but as he pleases, who alone is the possessor of heaven and earth, and the Lord of every creature. We have no right to dispose of anything we have, but according to his will, seeing as we are not proprietors of any of these things. They are all, as our Lord speaks, ἀλλοτρία, *belonging to another person;* nor is anything properly *our own,* in the land of our pilgrimage. We shall not receive τὰ ιδία, *our own things,* till we come to our own country. Eternal things only are our own; with all these temporal things we are barely entrusted by another, the Disposer and Lord of all. And he entrusts us with them on this express condition, that we use them only as our Master's goods, and according to the particular directions that he has given us in his Word.

2. On this condition he has entrusted us with our souls, our bodies, our goods, and whatever other talents we have received. But in order to impress this weighty truth on our hearts, it will be needful to come to particulars.

## We Have Been Entrusted with Our Souls

First, God has entrusted us with our soul, an immortal spirit, made in the image of God; together with all the powers and faculties thereof: understanding, imagination, memory, will, and a train of affections, either included in it or closely dependent upon it—love and hatred, joy and sorrow, respecting present good and evil; desire and aversion, hope and fear, respecting that which is to come. All these St. Paul seems to include in two words, when he says, "The peace of God shall keep your hearts and minds." Perhaps, indeed, the latter word, νοήματα, might rather be rendered *thoughts,* provided we take that word in its most extensive sense, for every perception of the mind, whether active or passive.

3. Now, of all these, it is certain, we are only stewards. God has entrusted us with these powers and faculties, not

that we may employ them according to our own will, but according to the express orders which he has given us; although it is true that, in doing his will, we most effectually secure our own happiness; seeing it is in this only that we can be happy, either in time or in eternity. Thus we are to use our understanding, our imagination, and our memory, wholly to the glory of him who gave them.

Thus our will is to be wholly given up to him, and all our affections to be regulated as he directs. We are to love and hate, to rejoice and grieve, to desire and shun, to hope and fear, according to the rule which he prescribes whose we are, and whom we are to serve in all things. Even our thoughts are not our own, in this sense; they are not at our own disposal; but for every deliberate motion of our mind we are accountable to our great Master.

## We Have Been Entrusted with Our Bodies

4. God has, secondly, entrusted us with our bodies (those exquisitely wrought machines, so "fearfully and wonderfully made"), with all the powers and members of it. He has entrusted us with the organs of sense; of sight, hearing, and the rest: but none of these are given us as our own, to be employed according to our own will. None of these are lent us in such a sense as to leave us at liberty to use them as we please for a season. No, we have received them on these very terms: that as long as they abide with us, we should employ them all in that very manner, and no other, which he appoints.

5. It is on the same terms that he has imparted to us that most excellent talent of speech. "You have given me a tongue," says the ancient writer, "that I may praise you with it." For this purpose it was given to all the children of men: to be employed in glorifying God. Nothing, therefore,

is more ungrateful or more absurd, than to think or say, "Our tongues are our own." That cannot be, unless we have created ourselves, and so are independent of the Most High. Moreover, but "it is he who has made us, and not we ourselves"; the manifest consequence is that he is still Lord over us, in this as in all other respects. It follows, that there is not a word of our tongue for which we are not accountable to him.

6. To him we are equally accountable for the use of our hands and feet, and all the members of our body. These are so many talents that are committed to our trust, until the time appointed by the Father. Until then, we have the use of all these; but as stewards, not as proprietors; to the end we should "render them, not as instruments of unrighteousness unto sin, but as instruments of righteousness unto God."

## We Have Been Entrusted with Worldly Goods

7. God has entrusted us, thirdly, with a portion of worldly goods; with food to eat, raiment to put on, and a place where we can lay our head; with not only the necessities, but the conveniences, of life. Above all, he has committed to our charge that precious talent which contains all the rest— money: indeed it is unspeakably precious, if we are wise and faithful stewards of it; if we employ every part of it for such purposes as our blessed Lord has commanded us to do.

## We Have Been Entrusted with Various Additional Gifts

8. God has entrusted us, fourthly, with several talents that do not properly come under any of these heads. Such is bodily strength; such are health, a pleasing person, an agreeable address; such are learning and knowledge, in their various degrees, with all the other advantages of education. Such is the influence that we have over others, whether by

their love and esteem of us, or by power—power to do them good or hurt, to help or hinder them in the circumstances of life. Add to these, that invaluable talent of time, with which God entrusts us from moment to moment. Add, lastly, that on which all the rest depend, and without which they would all be curses, not blessings; namely, the grace of God, the power of his Holy Spirit, which alone works in us all that is acceptable in his sight.

## II. The Time Is Swiftly Approaching When We "Can Be No Longer Stewards"

1. In so many respects are the children of men stewards of the Lord, the Possessor of heaven and earth: So large a portion of his goods, of various kinds, he has committed to their charge. But it is not forever, nor indeed for any considerable time. We have this trust reposed in us only during the short, uncertain space that we sojourn here below; only so long as we remain on earth, as this fleeting breath is in our nostrils. The hour is swiftly approaching; it is just at hand, when we "can be no longer stewards!"

The moment the body "returns to the dust as it was, and the spirit to God that gave it," we bear that character no more; the time of our stewardship is at an end. Part of those goods with which we were before entrusted are now come to an end; at least, they are so with regard to us; nor are we any longer entrusted with them: and that part which remains can no longer be employed or improved as it was before.

### We Have No More Portion under the Sun

2. Part of what we were entrusted with before is at an end, at least with regard to us. What have we to do, after this life, with food, and raiment, and houses, and earthly

possessions? The food of the dead is the dust of the earth; they are clothed only with worms and rottenness. They dwell in the house prepared for all flesh; their lands know them no more. All their worldly goods are delivered into other hands, and they have "no more portion under the sun."

3. The case is the same with regard to the body. The moment the spirit returns to God, we are no longer stewards of this machine, which is then sown in corruption and dishonor. All the parts and members of which it was composed lie moldering in the clay. The hands have no longer power to move; the feet have forgotten their office; the flesh, sinews, and bones are all hastening to be dissolved into common dust.

4. Here end also the talents of a mixed nature: our strength, our health, our beauty, our eloquence, and address, our faculty of pleasing or persuading, or convincing others. Here end, likewise, all the honors we once enjoyed, all the power which was lodged in our hands, all the influence which we once had over others, either by the love or the esteem which they bore us. Our love, our hatred, our desire, is perished: none regard how we were once affected toward them. They look upon the dead as neither able to help nor hurt them; so that "a living dog is better than a dead lion."

## Our Senses and Knowledge Will Remain and Flourish

5. Perhaps a doubt may remain concerning some of the other talents with which we are now entrusted, whether they will cease to exist when the body returns to dust or only cease to be improvable. Indeed, there is no doubt but the kind of speech that we now use, by means of these bodily organs, will then be entirely at an end, when those organs are destroyed. It is certain, the tongue will no more cause any vibrations in the air; neither will the ear convey these tremulous motions

to the common sensory. Even the *sonus exilis*, the low, shrill voice, which the poet supposes to belong to a separate spirit, we cannot allow to have a real being; it is a mere flight of imagination. Indeed, it cannot be questioned, but separate spirits have some way to communicate their sentiments to each other; but what inhabitant of flesh and blood can explain that way? What we term "speech," they cannot have; so that we can no longer be stewards of this talent when we are numbered with the dead.

6. It may be uncertain, whether our senses will exist, when the organs of sense are destroyed. Is it not probable, that those of the lower kind will cease—the feeling, the smell, the taste—as they have a more immediate reference to the body, and are chiefly, if not wholly, intended for the preservation of it? But will not some kind of sight remain, although the eye is closed in death? And will there not be something in the soul equivalent to the present sense of hearing? Moreover, is it not probable, that these will not only exist in the separate state, but exist in a far greater degree, in a more eminent manner than now, when the soul, disentangled from its clay, is no longer "a dying sparkle in a cloudy place"; when it no longer "looks through the windows of the eye and ear"; but rather is all eye, all ear, all sense, in a manner we cannot yet conceive?

And do we not have a clear proof of the possibility of this—of seeing without the use of the eye, and hearing without the use of the ear? Indeed, an earnest of it continually? For does not the soul see, in the clearest manner, when the eye is of no use; namely, in dreams? Does she not then enjoy the faculty of hearing, without any help from the ear? But however this be, certain it is, that neither will our senses, any more than our speech, be entrusted to us in the manner they are now, when the body lies in the silent grave.

7. How far the knowledge or learning that we have gained by education will then remain, we cannot tell. Solomon indeed says, "There is no work, nor device, nor knowledge, nor wisdom, in the grave, where you go." But it is evident; these words cannot be understood in an absolute sense. For it is so far from being true that there is no knowledge after we have quitted the body, that the doubt lies on the other side, whether there be any such thing as real knowledge till then; whether it be not a plain sober truth, not a mere poetical fiction, that

*All these shadows which for things we take,*
*Are but the empty dreams, which in death's sleep we make;*

only excepting those things which God himself has been pleased to reveal to man. I will speak for one. After having sought for truth, with some diligence, for half a century, I am, at this day, hardly sure of anything but what I learn from the Bible. Moreover, I positively affirm, I know nothing else so certainly, that I would dare to stake my salvation upon it.

So much, however, we may learn from Solomon's words, that "there is no" such "knowledge or wisdom in the grave," as will be of any use to an unhappy spirit; "there is no device" there, by which he can now improve those talents with which he was once entrusted. For time is no more; the time of our trial for everlasting happiness or misery is past. Our day, the day of man, is over; the day of salvation is ended! Nothing now remains but the "day of the Lord," ushering in wide, unchangeable eternity!

## Our Memory and Understanding Will Remain and Flourish

8. But still, our souls, being incorruptible and immortal, of a nature "little lower than the angels" (even if we are to

understand that phrase of our original nature, which may well be uncertain), when our bodies are moldered into earth, will remain with all their faculties. Our memory, our understanding, will be so far from being destroyed, indeed, or impaired, by the dissolution of the body, that, on the contrary, we have reason to believe, they will be inconceivably strengthened. Do we not have the clearest reason to believe that they will then be wholly freed from those defects that now naturally result from the union of the soul with the corruptible body?

It is highly probable, that, from the time these are disunited, our memory will let nothing slip; indeed, that it will faithfully exhibit everything to our view that was ever committed to it. It is true, that the invisible world is, in Scripture, termed "the land of forgetfulness"; or, as it is still more strongly expressed in the old translation, "the land where all things are forgotten." They are forgotten, but by whom? Not by the inhabitants of that land, but by the inhabitants of the earth. It is with regard to them that the unseen world is "the land of forgetfulness." All things in it are too frequently forgotten by these; but not by disembodied spirits. From the time they have put off the earthly tabernacle, we can hardly think they forget anything.

9. In like manner, the understanding will, doubtless, be freed from the defects that are now inseparable from it. For many ages it has been an unquestioned maxim: *Humanum est errare et nescire,* ignorance and mistake are inseparable from human nature. But the whole of this assertion is only true with regard to living men, and holds no longer than while "the corruptible body presses down the soul." Ignorance, indeed, belongs to every finite understanding (seeing there is none beside God who knows all things); but do not mistake: when the body is laid aside, this also is laid aside, forever.

10. What then can we say to an ingenious man, who has lately made a discovery, that disembodied spirits have not only no senses (not even sight or hearing), but no memory or understanding; no thought or perception; not so much as a consciousness of their own existence! That they are in a dead sleep from death to the resurrection! *Consanguineus lethi sopor* indeed! Such a sleep we may call "a near kinsman of death," if it be not the same thing. What can we say, but that ingenious men have strange dreams, and these they sometimes mistake for realities?

## Our Will and Affections Will Remain and Flourish

11. But to return. As the soul will retain its understanding and memory, notwithstanding the dissolution of the body, so undoubtedly the will, including all the affections, will remain in its full vigor. If our love or anger, our hope or desire, perish, it is only with regard to those whom we leave behind. To them it matters not, whether they were the objects of our love or hate, of our desire or aversion. But in separate spirits themselves we have no reason to believe that any of these are extinguished. It is more probable, that they work with far greater force, than while the soul was clogged with flesh and blood.

## But the Days of Our Stewardship Are Ended

12. But although all these, although both our knowledge and senses, our memory and understanding, together with our will, our love, hate, and all our affections, remain after the body is dropped off; yet, in this respect, they are as though they were not—we are no longer stewards of them. The things continue, but our stewardship does not: we no more act in that capacity. Even the grace that was formerly entrusted with us, in order to enable us to be faithful and

wise stewards, is now no longer entrusted for that purpose. The days of our stewardship are ended.

## III. We Must Give an Account of Our Stewardship

*We Will Appear Before the God and Judge of All*

1. It now remains, that, being no longer stewards, we give an account of our stewardship. Some have imagined this is to be done immediately after death, as soon as we enter into the world of spirits. Moreover, the Church of Rome does absolutely assert this; indeed, makes it an article of faith. And thus much we may allow, the moment a soul drops the body, and stands naked before God, it cannot but know what its portion will be to all eternity. It will have full in its view, either everlasting joy, or everlasting torment, as it is no longer possible to be deceived in the judgment which we pass upon ourselves. But the Scripture gives us no reason to believe, that God will then sit in judgment upon us. There is no passage in all the oracles of God that affirms any such thing.

That which has been frequently alleged for this purpose seems rather to prove the contrary; namely, "It is appointed for men once to die, and after this the judgment" (Heb. 9:27). For, in all reason, the word "once" is here to be applied to judgment as well as death. So that the fair inference to be drawn from this very text is, not that there are two judgments, a particular and a general; but that we are to be judged, as well as to die, once only: not once immediately after death, and again after the general resurrection; but then only "when the Son of man shall come in his glory, and all his holy angels with him." The imagination therefore of one judgment at death, and another at the end of the world, can

have no place with those who make the written Word of
God the whole and sole standard of their faith.

2. The time then when we are to give this account is
when the "great white throne comes down from heaven,
and he who sits on it, from whose face the heavens and the
earth flee away, and there is found no place for them." It
is then "the dead, small and great, will stand before God;
and the books will be opened"—the book of Scripture, to
them who were entrusted with it; the book of conscience to
all mankind. The "book of remembrance," likewise (to use
another scriptural expression), which had been writing from
the foundation of the world, will then be laid open to the
view of all the children of men.

Before all these, even the whole human race, before the
devil and his angels, before an innumerable company of holy
angels, and before God the Judge of all, you will appear,
without any shelter or covering, without any possibility of
disguise, to give a particular account of the manner in which
you have employed all your Lord's goods!

## We Must Account for the Souls Entrusted to Us

3. The Judge of all will then inquire, "How did you
employ your soul? I entrusted you with an immortal spirit,
endowed with various powers and faculties, with understanding, imagination, memory, will, affections. I gave you,
together with this, full and express directions, how all these
were to be employed. Did you employ your understanding,
as far as it was capable, according to those directions; namely,
in the knowledge of yourself and me—my nature, my attri-
butes? My works, whether of creation, of providence, or of
grace? In acquainting yourself with my word? In using every
means to increase your knowledge of it? In meditating on it
day and night?

"Did you employ your memory, according to my will, in treasuring up whatever knowledge you had acquired, which might conduce to my glory, to your own salvation, or the advantage of others? Did you store up in it, not things of no value, but whatever instruction you had learned from my word; and whatever experience you had gained of my wisdom, truth, power, and mercy? Was your imagination employed, not in painting vain images, much less such as nourished "foolish and hurtful desires"; but in representing to yourself whatever would profit your soul, and awaken your pursuit of wisdom and holiness?

"Did you follow my directions with regard to your will? Was it wholly given up to me? Was it swallowed up in mine, so as never to oppose, but always run parallel with it? Were your affections placed and regulated in such a manner, as I appointed in my word? Did you give me your heart? Did you not love the world, neither the things of the world? Was I the object of your love? Was all your desire unto me, and unto the remembrance of my name? Was I the joy of your heart, the delight of your soul, the chief among ten thousand? Did you sorrow for nothing, but what grieved my spirit? Did you fear and hate nothing but sin? Did the whole stream of your affections flow back to the ocean from which they came?

"Were your thoughts employed according to my will— not in ranging to the ends of the earth, not on folly, or sin; but on 'whatever things were pure, whatever things were holy'; on whatever was conducive to my glory, and to 'peace and goodwill among men'?"

## We Must Account for the Bodies Entrusted to Us

4. Your Lord will then inquire, "How did you employ the body with which I entrusted you? I gave you a tongue to praise me with: Did you use it to the end for which it

was given? Did you employ it, not in evil speaking or idle speaking, not in uncharitable or unprofitable conversation; but in such as was good, as was necessary or useful either to yourself or others? Such as always tended, directly or indirectly, to 'minister grace to the hearers'?

"I gave you, together with your other senses, those grand avenues of knowledge, sight, and hearing: Were these employed to those excellent purposes for which they were bestowed upon you? In bringing you in more and more instruction in righteousness and true holiness? I gave you hands and feet, and various members, with which to perform the works which were prepared for you: Were they employed, not in doing 'the will of the flesh,' of your evil nature; or the will of the mind (the things to which your reason or fancy led you); but 'the will of him who sent' you into the world, merely to work out your own salvation? Did you present all your members, not to sin, as instruments of unrighteousness, but to me alone, through the Son of my love, 'as instruments of righteousness'?"

## We Must Account for the Worldly Goods Entrusted to Us

5. The Lord of all will next inquire, "How did you employ the worldly goods which I lodged in your hands? Did you use your food, not so as to seek or place your happiness in it, but so as to preserve your body in health, in strength and vigor, a fit instrument for the soul? Did you use apparel, not to nourish pride or vanity, much less to tempt others to sin, but conveniently and decently to defend yourself from the injuries of the weather? Did you prepare and use your house, and all other conveniences, with a single eye to my glory—in every point seeking not your own honor, but mine; studying to please, not yourself, but me?

"Once more, in what manner did you employ that comprehensive talent, money? Not in gratifying the desire of the flesh, the desire of the eye, or the pride of life; not squandering it away in vain expenses—the same as throwing it into the sea; not hoarding it up to leave behind you—the same as burying it in the earth; but first supplying your own reasonable wants, together with those of your family; then restoring the remainder to me, through the poor, whom I had appointed to receive it; looking upon yourself as only one of that number of poor, whose wants were to be supplied out of that part of my substance which I had placed in your hands for this purpose; leaving you the right of being supplied first, and the blessedness of giving rather than receiving?

"Were you accordingly a general benefactor to mankind? Feeding the hungry, clothing the naked, comforting the sick, assisting the stranger, and relieving the afflicted, according to their various necessities? Were you eyes to the blind, and feet to the lame, a father to the fatherless, and an husband to the widow? And did you labor to improve all outward works of mercy, as means of saving souls from death?"

## We Must Account for the Additional Gifts Entrusted to Us

6. Your Lord will further inquire, "Have you been a wise and faithful steward with regard to the talents of a mixed nature which I lent you? Did you employ your health and strength, not in folly or sin, not in the pleasures that perished in the using, 'not in making provision for the flesh, to fulfill the desires of it,' but in a vigorous pursuit of that better part which none could take away from you?

"Did you employ whatever was pleasing in your person or address, whatever advantages you had by education, whatever share of learning, whatever knowledge of things or men was committed you, for the promoting of virtue in the world, for the enlargement of my kingdom? Did you employ whatever share of power you had, whatever influence over others, by the love or esteem of you that they had conceived, for the increase of their wisdom and holiness?

"Did you employ that inestimable talent of time, with wariness and circumspection, as duly weighing the value of every moment, and knowing that all were numbered in eternity? Above all, were you a good steward of my grace, preventing, accompanying, and following you?

"Did you duly observe, and carefully improve, all the influences of my Spirit—every good desire, every measure of light, all his sharp or gentle reproofs? How did you profit by 'the Spirit of bondage and fear,' which was previous to 'the Spirit of adoption'? And when you were made a partaker of this Spirit, crying in your heart, 'Abba, Father,' did you stand fast in the glorious liberty with which I made you free? Did you from then forth present your soul and body, all your thoughts, your words, and actions, in one flame of love, as a holy sacrifice, glorifying me with your body and your spirit?

"Then 'well done, good and faithful servant! Enter into the joy of your Lord!'"

And what will remain, either to the faithful or unfaithful steward? Nothing but the execution of that sentence which has been passed by the righteous Judge; fixing you in a state which admits of no change through everlasting ages! It remains only that you be rewarded, to all eternity, according to you works.

## IV. Implications

### Life Is Short and Uncertain

1. From these plain considerations we may learn, first, how important is this short, uncertain day of life! How

precious, above all utterance, above all conception, is every portion of it!

> *The least of these a serious care demands;*
> *For though they're little, they are golden sands!*

How deeply does it concern every child of man, to let none of these run to waste; but to improve them all to the noblest purposes, as long as the breath of God is in his nostrils!

## All We Do Is Either Good or Evil, Never Indifferent

2. We learn from this, secondly, that there is no employment of our time, no action or conversation, that is purely indifferent. All is good or bad, because all our time, as everything we have, is not our own. All these are, as our Lord speaks, τα ἀλλοτρία, *the property of another;* of God our Creator. Now, these either are, or are not, employed according to his will. If they are so employed, all is good; if they are not, all is evil.

Again, it is his will that we should continually grow in grace and in the living knowledge of our Lord Jesus Christ. Consequently, every thought, word, and work, by which this knowledge is increased, by which we grow in grace, is good; and every one by which this knowledge is not increased, is truly and properly evil.

## Everything Is from God, Everything Is Due God

3. We learn from this, thirdly, that there are no works of supererogation; that we can never do more than our duty; seeing all we have is not our own, but God's; all we can do is due to him. We have not received this or that, or many things only, but everything from him: therefore, everything is his due. He who gives us all has a right to all; so that if we pay him anything less than all, we cannot be faithful

stewards. And considering, "every man shall receive his own reward, according to his own labor," we cannot be wise stewards unless we labor to the uttermost of our power; not leaving anything undone that we possibly can do, but putting forth all our strength.

4. Brethren, "who is an understanding man and endued with knowledge among you?" Let him show the wisdom from above, by walking suitably to his character. If he so accounts himself as a steward of the manifold gifts of God, let him see that all his thoughts, and words, and works, be agreeable to the post God has assigned him. It is no small thing, to lay out for God all which you have received from God. It requires all your wisdom, all your resolution, all your patience and constancy; far more than ever you had by nature, but not more than you may have by grace. For his grace is sufficient for you, and "all things," you know, "are possible to him who believes." By faith, then, "put on the Lord Jesus Christ"; "put on the whole armor of God"; and you shall be enabled to glorify him in all your words and works; indeed, to bring every thought into captivity to the obedience of Christ!

# NINE

# The More
# Excellent Way

## 1787

*Covet earnestly the best gifts; and yet I show to you a more
excellent way.*

—1 Corinthians 12:31

## Introduction

### Covet the Extraordinary Gifts of the Spirit

1. In the preceding verses, St. Paul has been speaking of
the extraordinary gifts of the Holy Spirit; such as healing the
sick, prophesying (in the proper sense of the word; that is,
foretelling things to come), speaking with strange tongues,
such as the speaker had never learned, and the miraculous
interpretation of tongues. And these gifts the Apostle allows
to be desirable; indeed, he exhorts the Corinthians, at least
the teachers among them (to whom chiefly, if not solely, they
were wont to be given in the first ages of the Church) to *covet*

them *earnestly,* that thereby they might be qualified to be more useful either to Christians or heathens.

"And yet," he says, "I show unto you a more excellent way"; far more desirable than all these put together, so as it will infallibly lead you to happiness both in this world and in the world to come; whereas you might have all those gifts, indeed, in the highest degree, and yet be miserable both in time and eternity.

2. It does not appear that these extraordinary gifts of the Holy Spirit were common in the Church for more than two or three centuries. We seldom hear of them after that fatal period when the Emperor Constantine called himself a Christian, and from a vain imagination of promoting the Christian cause thereby heaped riches, and power, and honor upon the Christians in general, but in particular upon the Christian clergy. From this time they almost totally ceased; very few instances of the kind were found. The cause of this was not (as has been vulgarly supposed) "because there was no more occasion for them," because the entire world was become Christian. This is a miserable mistake; not a twentieth part of it was then nominally Christian.

The real cause was, "the love of many," almost of all, Christians, so called, was "waxed cold." The Christians had no more of the Spirit of Christ than the other heathens. The Son of Man, when he came to examine his Church, could hardly "find faith upon earth." This was the real cause of why the extraordinary gifts of the Holy Spirit were no longer to be found in the Christian Church—because the Christians were turned heathens again, and had only a dead form left.

## Covet the Ordinary Gifts of the Spirit

3. However, I would not at present speak of these, of the extraordinary gifts of the Holy Spirit, but of the ordinary;

and these likewise we may "covet earnestly," in order to be more useful in our generation. With this view we may covet "the gift of *convincing speech,*" in order to "sound the unbelieving heart"; and the gift of *persuasion,* to move the affections, as well as enlighten the understanding. We may covet *knowledge,* both of the word and of the works of God, whether of providence or grace. We may desire a measure of that *faith* which, on particular occasions, in which the glory of God or the happiness of men is nearly concerned, goes far beyond the power of natural causes. We may desire an easy elocution, a pleasing address, with resignation to the will of our Lord; indeed, whatever would enable us, as we have opportunity, to be useful wherever we are. These gifts we may innocently desire: but there is "a more excellent way."

### *Above All, Pursue "A More Excellent Way"*

4. The way of love—of loving all men for God's sake; of humble gentle, patient love—is that which the Apostle so admirably describes in the ensuing chapter. And without this, he assures us, all eloquence, all knowledge, all faith, all works, and all sufferings, are of no more value in the sight of God than sounding brass or a rumbling cymbal, and are not of the least avail toward our eternal salvation. Without this, all we know, all we believe, all we do, all we suffer, will profit us nothing in the great day of accounts.

### *An Alternate View of "A More Excellent Way"*

5. But at present I would take a different view of the text, and point out "a more excellent way" in another sense. It is the observation of an ancient writer that there have been from the beginning two orders of Christians. The one lived an innocent life, conforming in all things, not sinful, to the customs and fashions of the world; doing many good works,

abstaining from gross evils, and attending the ordinances of God. They endeavored, in general, to have a conscience void of offense in their outward behavior, but did not aim at any particular strictness, being in most things like their neighbors.

The other sort of Christian not only abstained from all appearance of evil, were zealous of good works in every kind, and attended all the ordinances of God, but also used all diligence to attain the whole mind that was in Christ, and labored to walk, in every point, as their beloved Master. In order to this they walked in a constant course of universal self-denial, trampling on every pleasure which they were not divinely conscious prepared them for taking pleasure in God. They took up their cross daily. They strove, they agonized without intermission, to enter in at the strait gate. This one thing they did: they spared no pains to arrive at the summit of Christian holiness; "leaving the first principles of the doctrine of Christ, to go on to perfection"; to "know all that love of God which passes knowledge, and to be filled with all the fullness of God."

6. From long experience and observation I am inclined to think, that whoever finds redemption in the blood of Jesus, whoever is justified, has then the choice of walking in the higher or the lower path. I believe the Holy Spirit at that time sets before him "the more excellent way," and incites him to walk in it, to choose the narrowest path in the narrow way, to aspire after the heights and depths of holiness, after the entire image of God. But if he does not accept this offer, he insensibly declines into the lower order of Christians. He still goes on in what may be called a good way, serving God in his degree, and finds mercy in the close of life, through the blood of the covenant.

7. I would be far from quenching the smoking flax, from discouraging those that serve God in a low degree. But I could not wish them to stop here: I would encourage them to come up higher, without thundering hell and damnation in their ears, without condemning the way in which they were—telling them it is the way that leads to destruction—I will endeavor to point out to them what is in every respect "a more excellent way."

8. Let it be well remembered: I do not affirm that all who do not walk in this way are in the high road to hell. But this much I must affirm, they will not have so high a place in heaven as they would have had if they had chosen the better part. And will this be a small loss, the having so many fewer stars in your crown of glory? Will it be a little thing to have a lower place than you might have had in the kingdom of your Father? Certainly there will be no sorrow in heaven; there all tears will be wiped from our eyes; but if it were possible grief could enter there, we should grieve at that irreparable loss. Irreparable then, but not now. Now, by the grace of God, we may choose the "more excellent way." Let us now compare this, in a few particulars, with the way in which most Christians walk.

## I. The More Excellent Way to Sleep

To begin at the beginning of the day. It is the manner of the generality of Christians, if they are not obliged to work for their living, to rise, particularly in winter, at eight or nine in the morning after having lain in bed eight or nine, if not more hours. I do not say now (as I should have been very apt to do fifty years ago) that all who indulge themselves in this manner are in the way to hell. But neither can I say they are in the way to heaven, denying themselves, and taking up their cross daily. Sure I am, there is "a more excellent way" to promote health both of body and mind.

From an observation of more than sixty years, I have learned, that men in health require, at an average, from six to seven hours of sleep, and healthy women a little more, from seven to eight, in four-and-twenty hours. I know this quantity of sleep to be most advantageous to the body as well as the soul. It is preferable to any medicine that I have known, both for preventing and removing nervous disorders. It is, therefore, undoubtedly the most excellent way, in defiance of fashion and custom, to take just so much sleep as experience proves our nature to require; seeing this is indisputably most conducive both to bodily and spiritual health.

And why should not you walk in this way? Because it is difficult? Indeed, with men it is impossible. But all things are possible with God; and by his grace all things will be possible to *you*. Only continue persistent in prayer, and you will find this not only possible, but easy: indeed, and it will be far easier to rise early constantly, than to do it sometimes. But then you must begin at the right end; if you rise early, you must sleep early. Impose it upon yourself, unless when something extraordinary occurs, to go to bed at a fixed hour. Then the difficulty of it will soon be over; but the advantage of it will remain forever.

## II. The More Excellent Way to Pray

The generality of Christians, as soon as they rise, are accustomed to use some kind of *prayer;* and probably to use the same form still which they learned when they were eight or ten years old. Now I do not condemn those who proceed thus (though many do) as mocking God; though they have used the same form, without any variation, for twenty or thirty years together. But surely there is "a more excellent way" of ordering our private devotions. What if you were to follow the advice given by that great and good man, Mr. Law, on this subject? Consider both your outward and inward state, and vary your prayers accordingly.

For instance: suppose your outward state is prosperous; suppose you are in a state of health, ease, and plenty, having your lot cast among kind relations, good neighbors, and agreeable friends, that love you and you them; then your outward state manifestly calls for praise and thanksgiving to God. On the other hand, if you are in a state of adversity; if God has laid trouble upon your loins; if you are in poverty, in want, in outward distress; if you are in any imminent danger; if you are in pain and sickness; then you are clearly called to pour out your soul before God in such prayer as is suited to your circumstances.

In like manner you may suit your devotions to your inward state, the present state of your mind. Is your soul in heaviness, either from a sense of sin, or through manifold temptations? Then let your prayer consist of such confessions, petitions, and supplications, as are agreeable to your distressed situation of mind. On the contrary, is your soul in peace? Are you rejoicing in God? Are his consolations not small with you? Then say, with the Psalmist: "You are my God, and I will love you: you are my God, and I will praise you." You may, likewise, when you have time, add to your other devotions a little reading and meditation, and perhaps a psalm of praise, the natural effusion of a thankful heart. You must certainly see that this is "a more excellent way" than the poor dry form that you used before.

## III. The More Excellent Way to Work

### To What End Do You Work?

1. The generality of Christians, after using some prayer, usually apply themselves to the *business* of their calling. Every man that has any pretense to be a Christian will not fail to do this; seeing it is impossible that an idle man can be a good man; sloth being inconsistent with religion. But with what view? To what end do you undertake and follow your worldly business? "To provide things necessary for myself and my family." It is a good answer as far as it goes; but it does not go far enough. For a Turk or a heathen goes so far, does his work for the very same ends.

But a Christian may go abundantly farther: his end in all his labor is to please God; to do, not his own will, but the will of him who sent him into the world—for this very purpose, to do the will of God on earth as angels do in heaven. He works for eternity. He "does not labor for the meat that perishes" (this is the smallest part of his motive), "but for that which endures to everlasting life." And is not this "a more excellent way"?

### In What Manner Do You Work?

2. Again, in what *manner* do you transact your worldly business? I trust, with diligence, whatever your hand finds to do, doing it with all your might; in justice, rendering to all their due, in every circumstance of life; indeed, and in mercy, doing unto every man what you wish he should do unto you. This is well: but a Christian is called to go still further, to add piety to justice; to intermix prayer, especially the prayer of the heart, with all the labor of his hands. Without this all his diligence and justice only show him to be an honest heathen;

and many there are who profess the Christian religion, that go no farther than honest heathenism.

## In What Spirit Do You Work?

3. Yet again: in what *spirit* do you go through your business—in the spirit of the world, or the Spirit of Christ? I am afraid thousands of those who are called good Christians do not understand the question. If you act in the Spirit of Christ you carry the end you at first proposed through all your work from first to last. You do everything in the spirit of sacrifice, giving up your will to the will of God; and continually aiming, not at ease, pleasure, or riches; not at anything "this short enduring world can give"; but merely at the glory of God. Now can anyone deny that this is the most excellent way of pursuing worldly business?

# IV. The More Excellent Way to Eat

## Eating with Thankfulness

1. But these tenements of clay which we bear about us require constant reparation, or they will sink into the earth from which they were taken, even sooner than nature requires. Daily food is necessary to prevent this, to repair the constant decays of nature. It was common in the heathen world when they were about to use this, to take meat or even drink, *libare pateram Jovi*, "to pour out a little to the honor of their god"; although the gods of the heathens were but devils, as the Apostle justly observes.

"It seems," says a late writer, "there was once some such custom as this in our own country. For we still frequently see a gentleman before he sits down to dinner in his own house, holding his hat before his face, and perhaps seeming to say something; though he generally does it in such a manner that no one can tell what he says." Now what if instead of this, every head of a family, before he sat down to eat and drink; morning, noon, or night (for the reason of the thing is the same at every hour of the day), was seriously to ask a blessing from God on what he was about to take? Indeed, and afterward, seriously to return thanks to the Giver of all his blessings? Would not this be "a more excellent way" than to use that dull farce which is worse than nothing; being, in reality, no other than mockery both of God and man?

2. As to the *quantity* of their food, good sort of men do not usually eat to excess. At least not so far as to make themselves sick with meat, or to intoxicate themselves with drink. And as to the manner of taking it, it is usually innocent, mixed with a little mirth, which is said to help digestion. So far, so good. And provided they take only that measure of plain, cheap, wholesome food, which most promotes health both of body and mind, there will be no cause of blame. Neither can I require you to take that advice of Mr. Herbert, though he was a good man:

> *Take thy meat; think it dust; then eat a bit*
> *And say with all, Earth to earth I commit.*

This is too melancholy: it does not suit with that cheerfulness which is highly proper at a Christian meal. Permit me to illustrate this subject with a little story. The King of France one day, pursuing the chase, outrode all his company, who after seeking him some time found him sitting in a cottage eating bread and cheese. Seeing them, he cried out: "Where have I lived all my time? I never before tasted so good food in my life!" "Sire," said one of them, "you never had so good sauce before; for you were never hungry."

Now it is true, hunger is a good sauce; but there is one that is better still; that is, thankfulness. Surely the most agreeable food is seasoned with this. And why should not yours be at every meal? You do not then need to cast your eye on death, but receive every morsel as a pledge of life eternal. The Author of your being gives you in this food, not only a reprieve from death, but an earnest that in a little time "death shall be swallowed up in victory."

## Eating with Right Conversation

3. The time of taking our food is usually a time of *conversation* also, as it is natural to refresh our minds while we refresh our bodies. Let us consider a little in what manner the generality of Christians usually converse together. What are the ordinary subjects of their conversation? If it is harmless (as one would hope it is), if there be nothing in it profane, nothing immodest, nothing untrue, or unkind; if there be no gossip, backbiting, or evil-speaking, they have reason to praise God for his restraining grace.

But there is more than this implied in "ordering our conversation aright." In order to do this, it is needful, first, that "your communication," that is, discourse or conversation, "be good"; that it be materially good, on good subjects; not fluttering about anything that occurs; for what have you to do with courts and kings? It is not your business to

*Fight over the wars, reform the state;*

unless when some remarkable event calls for the acknowledgment of the justice or mercy of God. We *must* indeed sometimes talk of worldly things; otherwise we may as well go out of the world. But it should only be so far as is needful; then we should return to a better subject. Secondly, let your conversation be "to the use of edifying"; calculated to edify either the speaker or the hearers, or both; to build them up, as each has particular need, either in faith, or love, or holiness. Thirdly, see that it not only gives entertainment, but, in one kind or other, "ministers grace to the hearers." Now, is not this "a more excellent way" of conversing than the harmless way above-mentioned?

# V. The More Excellent Way to Enjoy Diversions

1. We have seen what is the "more excellent way" of ordering our conversation, as well as our business. But we cannot be always intent upon business: both our bodies and minds require some relaxation. We need intervals of diversion from business. It will be necessary to be very explicit upon this head, as it is a point that has been much misunderstood.

## Matters of Conscience

2. Diversions are of various kinds. Some are almost peculiar to men, as the sports of field hunting, shooting, fishing, in which not many women (I should say, ladies) are concerned. Others are indifferently used by persons of both sexes; some of which are of a more public nature, as races, masquerades, plays, assemblies, balls. Others are chiefly used in private houses, as cards, dancing, and music; to which we may add the reading of plays, novels, romances, newspapers, and fashionable poetry.

3. Some diversions indeed that were formerly in great request are now fallen into disrepute. The nobility and gentry (in England at least) seem totally to disregard the once fashionable diversion of hawking; and the vulgar themselves are no longer diverted by men hacking and hewing each other

in pieces at broad-sword. The noble game of quarter-staff, likewise, is now exercised by very few. Indeed, cudgeling has lost its honor, even in Wales itself. Bear-baiting also is now very seldom seen, and bull-baiting not very often. And it seems cock-fighting would totally cease in England, were it not for two or three right honorable patrons.

4. It is not needful to say anything more of these foul *remains of Gothic barbarity,* than that they are a reproach, not only to all religion, but even to human nature. One would not pass so severe censure on the sports of the field. Let those who have nothing better to do, still run foxes and hares out of breath. Neither need much be said about horseraces, till some man of sense will undertake to defend them.

It seems a great deal more may be said in defense of seeing a serious tragedy. I could not do it with a clear conscience; at least not in an English theatre, the sink of all profaneness and debauchery; but possibly others can. I cannot say quite so much for balls or assemblies, which are more reputable than masquerades, but must be allowed by all impartial persons to have exactly the same tendency. So undoubtedly have all public dancing. And the same tendency they must have, unless the same caution obtained among modern Christians that was observed among the ancient heathens. With them men and women never danced together, but always in separate rooms. This was always observed in ancient Greece, and for several ages at Rome, where a woman dancing in company with men would have at once been set down for a prostitute.

Of playing at cards I say the same as of seeing plays. I could not do it with a clear conscience. But I am not obliged to pass sentences on those that are otherwise minded. I leave them to their own Master: to him let them stand or fall.

## *Opportunities for Ministry and Prayer*

5. But supposing these, as well as the reading of plays, novels, newspapers, and the like, to be quite innocent diversions; yet are there not more excellent ways of diverting themselves for those that love or fear God? Would men of fortune divert themselves in the open air? They may do it by cultivating and improving their lands, by planting their grounds, by laying out, carrying on, and perfecting their gardens and orchards. At other times they may visit and converse with the most serious and sensible of their neighbors; or they may visit the sick, the poor, the widows, and fatherless in their affliction.

Do they desire to divert themselves in the house? They may read useful history, pious and elegant poetry, or several branches of natural philosophy. If you have time, you may divert yourself by music, and perhaps by philosophical experiments. But above all, when you have once learned the use of prayer, you will find that as

> *That which yields or fills*
> *All space, the ambient air, wide interfused*
> *Embraces round this florid earth;*

so will this, till through every space of life it be interfused with all your employments, and wherever you are, whatever you do, embrace you on every side. Then you will be able to say boldly:

> *With me no melancholy void,*
> *No moment lingers unemploy'd,*
> *Or unimproved below:*
> *My weariness of life is gone,*
> *Who live to serve my God alone,*
> *And only Jesus know.*

# VI. The More Excellent Way to Steward Money

One point only remains to be considered; that is, the use of money. What is the way in which the generality of Christians employ this? And is there not "a more excellent way"?

## Basic Tithing

1. The generality of Christians usually set apart something yearly—perhaps a tenth or even one-eighth part of their income, whether it arise from yearly revenue, or from trade—for charitable uses. Few I have known who said like Zaccheus, "Lord, the half of my goods I give to the poor." O that it would please God to multiply these friends of mankind, these general benefactors!

2. Besides those who have a stated rule, there are thousands who give large sums to the poor; especially when any striking instance of distress is represented to them in lively colors.

3. I praise God for all of you who act in this manner. May you never be weary of well doing! May God restore what you give sevenfold into your own bosom! But yet I show unto you a more excellent way.

## True Stewards

4. You may consider yourself as one in whose hands the Proprietor of heaven and earth and all things therein has lodged a part of his goods, to be disposed of according to his direction. And his direction is, that you should look upon yourself as one of a certain number of indigent persons who are to be provided for out of that portion of his goods with which you are entrusted. You have two advantages over the rest: The one, that "it is more blessed to give than to receive"; the other, that you are to serve yourself first, and others afterwards. This is the light in which you are to see yourself

and them. But to be more particular: first, if you have no family, after you have provided for yourself, give away all that remains; so that

> *Each Christmas your accounts may clear,*
> *And wind your bottom round the year.*

This was the practice of all the young men at Oxford who were called Methodists. For example, one of them had thirty pounds a year. He lived on twenty-eight and gave away forty shillings. The next year receiving sixty pounds, he still lived on twenty-eight, and gave away two-and-thirty. The third year he received ninety pounds, and gave away sixty-two. The fourth year he received a hundred and twenty pounds. Still he lived as before on twenty-eight; and gave to the poor ninety-two. Was not this a more excellent way?

Secondly, if you have a family, seriously consider before God, how much each member of it wants, in order to have what is needful for life and godliness. And in general, do not allow them less, neither much more, than you allow yourself.

Thirdly, this being done, fix your purpose, to "gain no more." I charge you in the name of God, do not increase your substance! As it comes daily or yearly, so let it go: otherwise you "lay up treasures upon earth." And this our Lord as flatly forbids as murder and adultery. By doing it, therefore, you would "treasure up to yourselves wrath against the day of wrath and revelation of the righteous judgment of God."

## Lay Up Treasure in Heaven

5. But suppose it were not forbidden, how can you on principles of reason spend your money in a way which God may *possibly forgive*, instead of spending it in a manner which he will *certainly reward*? You will have no reward in heaven for what you *lay up*; you will, for what you *lay out*. Every

pound you put into the earthly bank is sunk: it brings no interest above. But every pound you give to the poor is put into the bank of heaven. And it will bring glorious interest; indeed, and such as will be accumulating to all eternity.

6. Who then is a wise man, and endued with knowledge among you? Let him resolve this day, this hour, this moment, the Lord assisting him, to choose in all the preceding particulars the "more excellent way"; and let him steadily keep it, both with regard to sleep, prayer, work, food, conversation, and diversions; and particularly with regard to the employment of that important talent, money. Let *your* heart answer to the call of God, "From this moment, God being my helper, I will lay up no more treasure upon earth. This one thing I will do, I will lay up treasure in heaven; I will render unto God the things that are God's; I will give him all my goods, and all my heart."